About the Author

'Father, I cannot tell a lie, I did it with my littl…
George Washington

Graham Jones, who is 27 this year, was bo…
Yorkshire. As a young man he joined the SA…
before graduating from Harvard, Yale, Prin…
and the Monetarist School. He became a fu…
Tonguester during spells in the Buckingham…
and as a speech-writer to Mr Denis Healey. T…
President of the Tommy Docherty Appreciation Society, he recalls being trapped in a lift with Russell Harty as his most embarrassing moment. The person he most wants to meet – alive or dead – is Fidel Castro. In his spare time he practises cardiovascular surgery and is a fully qualified astronaut. This is his 10,003rd book; of the other 10,002, *Forked Tongues: the (Original) Book of Lies, Half-truths and Excuses* and *Own Goals* have been published.

What They Said About Forked Tongues

'a treasury of fibs, whitewash and egg-all-over-my-face remarks'
Daily Mail

'a book of delightful disillusionment'
Sunday Telegraph

'Graham Jones leaves no newspaper unturned in his quest for gems'
Mail on Sunday

'a marvellous miscellany of mendacity'
Western Morning News

'but how do we know *he's* telling the truth?'
Sunday Times

Illustrated by Bill Belcher

THE FORKED TONGUES ANNUAL

GRAHAM JONES

CENTURY PUBLISHING
LONDON

Acknowledgements

The author wouldn't really like to thank anyone, because he's mean like that. But, mostly because his lawyer insists, he would like to put on record his profound gratitude to the publishers of all Britain's national newspapers and magazines (which he takes religiously, with the exception of the *Church Times*, which he takes from the local library reading room – as long as he can get there first) and to the publishers of America's four leading magazines, not to mention a plethora of British and American publishers too numerous to mention.

A special thanks to Professor Jerald Jellison of the University of Southern California for suggesting material on the mechanics and psychology of lying.

But most of all, to the Forked Tonguesters quoted without whom . . . he wouldn't have made any money out of this.

First published in Great Britain in 1985
by Century Hutchinson Ltd,
Brookmount House, 62–65 Chandos Place, London WC2N 4NW

ISBN 0 7126 1060 X

Designed by Gwyn Lewis

Typeset by Rowland Phototypesetting Ltd,
Bury St Edmunds, Suffolk
Printed and bound by R J Acford Ltd, Chichester, Sussex

Contents

YOU SCRATCH MY BACK AND I'LL SCRATCH YOURS

1 FORKED TONGUES REVIEW OF THE YEAR

Following the record-breaking, epoch-making, sensational, totally unprecedented, runaway success of *Forked Tongues*, the publishers in their wisdom and not unnatural desire for still more money asked me to come up with *The Forked Tongues Annual*, looking specifically at the lies, half-truths and excuses of the last sixteen months.

Here, in one magnificent volume, are the falsehoods, the fibs, the half-truths, the alibis and the evasions of the powerful, the rich and the famous during the year April 1984 to July 1985.

Actually, I lied there. I extended the period to take in the start of the miners' strike, on March 10, 1984, the date which saw the beginning of one of the most prolonged exercises in lies, deception and doubletalk – on all three sides – for years.

So, what sort of a year has it been for *aficionados* of the silky sleight of tongue, the elaborate false trail, the carefully schemed political cover-up? In a word: unbelievable! You might even say that 1984, the year of Orwellian portent, was in itself the year of the lie – even if it did continue into 1985!

APRIL

Mr Marat Gramov, president of the Soviet national Olympic committee, declares that his country *will* be at Los Angeles: 'There will be no Soviet boycott. The problems we have been discussing have been of a major nature, but we have now reached agreement.'

The *Globe*, an American newspaper, reports that the Queen will abdicate within 12 months 'to stop Charles and Diana quarrelling'. Bucketfuls of tears were shed, says the tabloid, at a poignant meeting between the Queen and the Princess to work out details of the succession.

MAY Arthur Scargill tells the BBC *Today* programme, 'I know of no violence by striking miners.'

Mrs Thatcher says: 'We are not going to intervene in the coal dispute.'

George Best declares from California: 'I have never been more together in my life.'

JUNE President Mitterrand bravely raises the case of Andrei Sakharov at a Kremlin dinner and President Chernenko tells him drily: 'Those who are trying to give us advice about human rights can only cause an ironic smile here.'

John McEnroe tells the press at Wimbledon: 'I'm not going to change the world. But if I can make people a bit happier, that's good enough for me.'

JULY Mrs Cristina De Lorean creates a stir by her stunning appearance in court every day in Los Angeles in support of her husband who is facing cocaine-smuggling charges. She says: 'Look, my life is with this man. I can't imagine it without him. Doesn't anyone understand about love any more?' (They split up almost immediately afterwards.)

Mr Gary Susnjara of North Carolina puts on the market 'An Alien in a Can' at $5 a time. Each can contains a 4½-inch-high visitor from the planet Mung. The can is labelled: 'Do not puncture this can: Alien will die and disappear.'

Eighteen-stone 'clairvoyant' actor Ken Parry is awarded a centre-page spread in the *Daily Star* and dubbed: 'The man with the gift'. He is asked in half-inch-high print: 'And what about the sex of Charles and Di's forthcoming baby?' 'Obviously it will be a girl,' says Ken.

AUGUST

A brazen French liar called Eric Capelli of Lyons announces he is offering a 'rent-a-lie' service at £5 a time. For that small fee he declares himself available for making excuses for business blunders, and lying smoothly to all manner of customers.

Postwoman Mrs Betty Kilbane, 47, is told to 'hop it' at Cardiff Crown Court, after claiming that a fall on her daily rounds had left her with a limp and permanent pain. A film shot by a private detective while she was out shopping showed her walking perfectly normally.

An anonymous BBC Radio 4 sports commentator at the Los Angeles Olympics comes out with the classic: 'And Britain defeats the rest of the world to pick up the bronze medal.'

SEPTEMBER

Defector Oleg Bitov appears at a Moscow press conference. He *had* said: 'I hope that with the help of world opinion those who are nearest and dearest to me will be able sooner or later to get out of the Soviet Union to join me.' Now, with the help of notes passed to him by a Soviet official, he claims: 'As I returned to my hotel, I stepped into the darkness only to get a terrible blow at the back of the head . . . for the rest of my days in Italy I was half-conscious . . . the psychotropic injections had done their job well . . .' Not to mention the KGB.

He is still unable to explain how he had acquired a suntan while in the West . . . it seems he'd managed a holiday at a four-star hotel in North Africa while being 'subjected to drugs, psychological treatment, violence and torture'.

OCTOBER

The *Guardian* reveals the most astounding lie of the year: Church of England clergy have been faking their attendance returns so that they don't have to pay as much of their collection money to the diocesan authorities. What *is* the world coming to?

The Reagan *v.* Mondale TV debates get under way with a welter of lies and superbluff. Mr Reagan says he had never claimed nuclear missiles fired from submarines could be recalled (he had, in May 1982); he says proposals to the Soviets at Geneva for first-phase reductions had not included submarine weapons (they had); he says the Carter–Mondale administration had supported unilateral disarmament (in their last year, they stepped up arms spending).

Mr Mondale enters into the spirit of things with some startlingly unfactual statements about the safety of US marines in Lebanon, and says the Reagan 'Star Wars' weapons programme is swallowing up $30 billion a year; actually the figure is $1.3 billion. But who cares about facts?

NOVEMBER

Labour leader Neil Kinnock claims his 'diary is full' so he cannot appear at rallies supporting the miners' strike.

In New Hampshire, a forger jailed for passing off his cheque book as belonging to Senator Edward Kennedy's son and magnate Armand Hammer's grandson proves that prison doesn't necessarily reform the compulsive liar. He springs himself from jail by forging a judge's signature on bogus release papers.

DECEMBER

BBC Director General Alastair Milne pleads for a £65 TV licence – a 41 per cent rise – despite revelations of a wasteful first-class junket to Hong Kong by senior executives and their wives. Milne stretches incredulity further by calling the £65 licence 'the best bargain in Britain' and claims: 'The public will recognise that it's value for money.'

Hundreds of Americans are tricked into sending $40 for a 'cabbage patch', thinking they would get the much-sought-after children's doll. All they receive from two

Florida conmen who placed the ads are . . . a packet of cabbage seeds and instructions on how to sow your own 'patch'.

JANUARY

Arthur Scargill says: 'We have got 140,000 men on strike. The Coal Board have requested talks. We are going into talks without preconditions. What on earth are you talking about defeat for?'

Svetlana Peters, Stalin's daughter, who had said that the Bolshevik revolution was 'a fatal, tragic mistake', that her father was 'a monster', that the Soviet system was 'profoundly corrupt', and that the KGB were 'like the German Gestapo', turns up at a KGB-sponsored press conference in Moscow and announces: 'I did not enjoy one single day of freedom in the West.'

Gossip columnist Kit Miller reveals he is the man in the life of Miss Samantha Fox, 17, the *Sun*'s extravagantly chested 'Page Three girl of the year'. He says: 'When I first met Sam, I didn't think, "Cor Blimey, what big knockers." I didn't even notice, honest.' A rival columnist says of Mr Miller, who is twice the age of the young blonde: 'His eyesight must have gone.'

Encouraged by her mother, 17-year-old 34DD-cup model Miss Debee Ashby flies off from her Hertfordshire home to join actor Tony Curtis at his Palm Springs mansion. Says Mrs Ashby: 'All they do is talk about art galleries, museums and life. He takes her out to candlelight dinners, because he doesn't want to be seen in flashy nightclubs. So that means he is a sincere person.' Says Debee on her return: 'I don't think he asked me out there because of my big boobs. He said he thought I had a very interesting personality.'

FEBRUARY

There is a furore after leaking civil servant Clive Ponting is acquitted on a secrets charge. Margaret Thatcher, Defence Secretary Michael Heseltine, Armed Forces Minister John Stanley and Attorney General Sir Michael Havers all tell how by an odd coincidence they were all on holiday when the decision to prosecute Mr Ponting was taken. Neil Kinnock says of the Prime Minister's denial of involvement: 'Frankly, I do not believe the Right Honourable Lady.' Not that he is calling her a liar, you understand. Later he apologises.

Meanwhile it is revealed hunky actor Stacy Keach, in jail on a drugs charge, has been allowed his own cell, a typewriter, extra female visitors and the privilege of missing exercise sessions, and that he is addressed by warders as 'Mr Keach'. A Home Office spokesman admits all this but says: 'Mr Keach is treated no differently to any other prisoner.'

MARCH

The miners' strike ends and Arthur Scargill flies to Moscow. He tells the Soviet trades-union daily, *Trud*: 'The NUM has won a brilliant victory.'

Ronald Reagan, it is revealed, has gone stereo with a second hearing aid. Dr John House, presidential physician, denies that the President's hearing is getting worse. Larry Speakes, White House press secretary, says: 'It is to balance sounds.'

A left-wing lecturer turned author reveals that Baron Gunther von Reibnitz, father of Princess Michael, was a member of the SS. Princess Michael tells TV-am of her 'shock' as she 'suddenly discovered something that really is quite unpleasant'. There is much debate as to whether she, or the Royal Family, knew in advance. One newspaper poll shows the Princess is just as popular as ever, but that two-thirds believe there was a cover-up. Interestingly enough, the first Buckingham Palace statement talks of the Princess's 'shock at hearing of the revelations', not at her 'shock at hearing of the facts'. Where Buckingham Palace firmly overstep the mark, however, is by insisting: 'there will be no further public statement'. Within hours, the Princess gives a full interview to TV-am's Nick Owen.

APRIL

Runner Anthony Chandler is stripped of his gold medal for winning the Wolverhampton marathon after race marshals report 'conclusive evidence' that he had cheated. Onlookers report seeing him slip into a crowd of leading runners just before the finishing line, and officials confirm that they have no record of his having passed the 10-, 15- or 25-mile points.

Irishman Michael Cash is fined £150 by Brighton magistrates for speeding and drink-driving after offering the memorable excuse: 'I'm hurrying home because I have a flat tyre and want to get there before it does down.'

Mrs Margaret Thatcher forgets where she is. She tells a large audience in Jakarta, Indonesia: 'We are all impressed by the way President Suharto and his Cabinet are handling the problems of Malaysia.' She had left Malaysia three days before. Later on her trip, asked a question about Prime Minister Lee Kuan Yew of Singapore, she replies: 'We do not have any bilateral problems with Hong Kong.'

MAY

Arthur Scargill declares: 'If anyone believes the miners have been defeated they are living in cloud cuckoo land.'

The *Sun* treats its readers to an entertaining form guide to contestants in the Eurovision Song Contest, by Charles Catchpole. The Belgian entry, 'Let Me Go Now', by Linda Lepomme is described thus: 'A touch of class here. A stark and simple love song, beautifully sung by an elegant blonde. My rating: Just watch it go.' The song finished 19th out of 19 entries, with just seven points.

Alan Thompson, billed as 'Tommo, the Voice of Sport' in the *Daily Express*, gets jingoistic on the eve of the Scotland *v.* England soccer international: 'Of course England will thrash them out of sight . . . as an all-round side England are far better than Scotland. In fact, England's second team could probably beat Scotland.' England – first team – lose 1–0.

JUNE Shi'ite terrorist hijackers who kick and pistol-whip an American to the point of death, then shoot him through the head before dumping him on the Beirut airport tarmac, are described by Demis Roussos, singer and a released hostage, as 'very nice people'. 'I spent some very good moments,' says Mr Roussos, who sang songs to his captors. 'These people looked after me in a way you cannot imagine.'

JULY President Regan has two feet of intestine removed in a tough three-hour operation. Although independent medical experts point to the seriousness of the surgery, Mr Reagan announces he is 'fit as a fiddle'. His aides go further. They describe him as '99.9 per cent fit' shortly before cancer is admitted. The *Daily Mirror* hits the nail on the head: 'If his doctors are to be believed, President Reagan combines the best of Flash Gordon, Superman, Dick Barton and Billy the Kid. So many superlatives flow, he sounds like a man with Heineken in his veins instead of blood.'

2 THE FORKED TONGUES OF THE YEAR AWARDS

1 **BLACK LIE OF THE YEAR:** *Gerry Adams*, President of Sinn Fein, talking on the attempt to murder Margaret Thatcher and other cabinet ministers at the Grand Hotel, Brighton: 'This was not a blow against democracy. It was a blow for democracy.'

2 **THE TOMMY DOCHERTY FORKED TONGUES LONG-SERVICE AWARD:** *James Baker*, Chief of Staff, the White House, who in December 1984 vehemently denied he would soon be on the move from his post, saying: 'I'm sticking around, time undetermined.' Within a fortnight he had completed a job-switch with Treasury Secretary Donald Regan.

3 **BRITISH POLITICAL BLUFF OF THE YEAR:** *Mr Chris Butler*, Conservative candidate on his way to a mauling (and the halving of the Tory vote) in the Brecon and Radnor by-election who said: 'My reception on the doorstep has been very warm. I don't get the impression this is a volatile seat like Portsmouth South or Orpington and that the vote will flip over to the Liberals. If anything, my vote is hardening.' The *Daily Mirror* publish a MORI poll on the day of the Brecon and Radnor by-election showing Labour with an 18 per cent lead and claim 'a Labour landslide'. 'When we win here we will change the course of British history,' says Mr Michael Foot, visiting the constituency and reawakening memories of the party's 1983 defeat. Despite a claimed 3 per cent margin of error, MORI are 19.5 per cent out on the result, a narrow win for Liberal–Alliance candidate Mr Richard Livsey.

4 INTERNATIONAL LIE OF THE YEAR: *Colonel Muammar Gaddafi* of Libya who, on April 18, 1984, after the gunning down of WPC Yvonne Fletcher from inside the People's Bureau in St James's Square, said: 'British policemen killed her because they attacked our bureau together with a group of Libyan terrorists, supported by aeroplanes and helicopters.'

5 SHOWBUSINESS LIE OF THE YEAR: *Katie Rabett*, model girlfriend of Prince Andrew, who on May 18, 1984, at the Cannes Film Festival announced: 'The publicity over my friendship with Prince Andrew was disastrous for my career. It almost finished me. I virtually had to start all over again.' Later she admitted that she was being offered up to £15,000 for a photo session . . . *after* the publicity about her and the Prince. Earnings of Katie, 23, for the year were later estimated to be £100,000.

It was Miss Rabett's second big bluff of the year. In March 1984, after nude pictures allegedly of her turned up in a Sunday newspaper, she said: 'I can categorically say that those two nude photographs are fakes. I have never posed nude either professionally or for friends.' After legal action was threatened she changed her story . . . the pictures were genuine. She 'just couldn't remember them being taken'.

6 POP FORKED TONGUESTER OF THE YEAR: *Simon Le Bon* of Duran Duran, who told an interviewer from *Woman* magazine in May 1984: 'I'm not a snob. Ask anybody. Well . . . anybody who matters.'

7 THE MICHAEL FAGAN AWARD FOR BEING ABSOLUTELY BEASTLY TO A MEMBER OF THE ROYAL FAMILY: *Peter Byfield*, manager of a shady establishment called 'School Dinners Restaurant', who claimed after a visit by Prince Andrew in June 1984: 'Three of my schoolgirl waitresses held him down while the lovely Sonia whipped him with a cane.' After Palace protests, Mr Byfield admitted that the incident had never happened.

8 SPECIAL BLACK NUTTY SLACK AWARD FOR LIES DURING THE COAL STRIKE: *Arthur Scargill* (who else?), not least for his observation in the *Observer* in August 1984: 'We run our union democratically. If we decide we want a ballot, we have one.'

9 LIES, DAMNED LIES . . . THE STATISTICAL FABRICATION OF THE YEAR AWARD: *Nigel Lawson*, Chancellor of the Exchequer, for claiming in the House of Commons on August 6, 1984, that the pits strike had 'probably added, net, some £300 to £400 million to public expenditure so far this year.' But four weeks earlier, on July 6, he had already put the figure at £400 million. Had the strike started to *make* money?

Other independent economists poured scorn on the Chancellor's figures, suggesting the strike might really be costing £240 million a month (city analysts Simon and Coates) or, by the time of the Chancellor's '£300 to £400 million' statement, some £1200 million. In his March 1985 Budget Lawson admitted to figures of £2500 million added to public expenditure (implying a figure of around £1000 million by August 6), with £4000 million added to the balance of payments deficit and a £2750 million increase in government borrowing.

10 THE HAROLD WILSON AWARD FOR PRIME MINISTERIAL IMAGINATION-STRETCHING: *Mrs Margaret Thatcher*, for her remark to George Gale in June

1984, on the miners' strike: 'I really do not see any role for Government intervention.'

11 THE 'YES MINISTER' KCMG FOR BOGUS DENIALS BY GOVERNMENT SPOKESMEN: The unidentified spokesman for Mrs Thatcher, who in January 1985, misled every Sunday paper except the *Observer* (the only one sensible enough not to believe him) by saying the government would not prop up the plummeting pound: 'You can be absolutely certain that we are not going to throw money at the pound. We are not going to defend a particular parity.' By the time the papers hit the streets, the dramatic U-turn had already been made.

12 SPORTS FORKED TONGUESTER OF THE YEAR: *John McEnroe*, who after hurling abuse at an umpire in a pre-Wimbledon tournament, in June 1984, plucked his racket strings moodily through a press conference and declared: 'I have always been one for constructive criticism.'

13 BUSINESS VOICE OF THE YEAR: *Robert Maxwell*, who took over the *Daily Mirror* in July 1984 promising: 'I will not interfere editorially' – except, he said, for an occasional hand on the tiller. For the rest of the year, a picture of the beaming new press magnate was barely off the front page . . . or the back page . . . or page two . . . or . . . Indeed, evidence of proprietorial interference ran riot in what came to be known as the *Daily Maxwell*.

14 TV LIE OF THE YEAR: *Joan Collins*, for claiming in an interview in April 1984: 'I would rather die than watch an episode of *Dynasty*.'

15 SPECIAL AWARD FOR FORKED TONGUESTERS IN HOLY ORDERS: *Reverend David Jenkins*, the Bishop of Durham, for his claim about a family in Sunderland living on £9.48 social security a day: 'The two sons, aged 10 and 12, have to take turns to go to school as they only have one pair of shoes between them.' He added for good measure: 'There are probably tens of thousands of such cases.' The figures were denied by the DHSS. The family – or even one of the 'tens of thousands' – couldn't be found.

16 U-TURN OF THE YEAR: *Paul Nicholas*, alias Vince Pinner of the TV series *Just Good Friends*. Throughout the success of the show in 1984, he told why he would not be marrying his live-in girlfriend Linzi Jennings: 'I'm a lot like Vince. I'm not crazy about marriage. I think it changes people for the worse. I think a woman finds a man more attractive if she can never quite nail him down.' Within hours of one such interview in December, they wed at Wood Green register office to headlines proclaiming: 'VINCE IN "I DO" SHOCK.' Said 'Vince': 'It is difficult to explain why we got married. It just seemed the natural thing to do.'

17 PRESIDENTIAL BLARNEY OF THE YEAR: *Ronald Reagan* for his statement on his rain-lashed visit to a one-donkey village to trace his Irish heritage: 'I can't think of a place on this planet I would rather claim as my roots than Ballyporeen, County Tipperary.'

18 EXCUSE OF THE YEAR: Award shared between Democratic presidential-race losers *Walter Mondale* ('I never really warmed up to TV, and it never really warmed up to me') and *Geraldine Ferraro* ('I feel Rupert Murdoch cost me the election'). *Nobody* warmed up to Mondale – it wasn't just TV. As for Rupert Murdoch losing a candidate 49 states, let's hope Robert Maxwell wasn't listening.

19 THE JOAN COLLINS AWARD FOR FALSE MODESTY: *Clint Eastwood*, who told a magazine in May 1984: 'I never see myself as a sex symbol. It's just that I'm sensitive to light and I squint a lot.'

20 CRAZIEST FORKED TONGUESTER OF THE YEAR: *Teddy Beverley* of the Beverley Sisters, who during the year made a sensational and glittering comeback as the darlings of the gay club circuit. She says: 'The Beverley Sisters were the Frankie Goes to Hollywood of the 'fifties.' The mind boggles!

3 THAT'S SHOWBIZ!

'To be a fine actor,' said George Burns, 'you've got to be honest. And if you can fake that – well, you've got it made.'

After politicians, showbiz types just have to be the most dishonest in the world. It's not just that actors and actresses spend their lives deceiving us that they're really somebody else. The dream factory, to become what it was, had to act as the lie factory as well. It's even got its own killer disease: terminal insincerity.

I get shot, Cliff Barnes gets shot, Sue Ellen gets shot, and so does li'l ol' Bobby.

Larry Hagman, mischievously to reporters, May 1984. Only Bobby got the bullet

---

It's just like being a very highly paid soldier.

Michael Caine on film-making, June 1984

Hollywood publicity handouts are known for telling the untruth, and nothing like the truth. Arnold Schwarzennegger's biography from the studio reported that he had been a weak, sickly child, always in the shadow of his elder brother, but that at the age of 15 he had rebelled against being a schoolboy weakling and discovered body-building. Said our hero as an adult:

That is a load of rubbish. I never told them such things. I was always a healthy child.

And it's not just Hollywood:

People think that working on *Coronation Street* is a doddle. All I can say is that it is hell.

Fred Feast, barman Fred Gee in the famous ITV soap opera

You know these TV series. In February 1985 tough guy Michael Brandon of *Dempsey and Makepeace* moaned in the *Daily Star*, under the headline MICHAEL'S LOVE LIFE IS ARRESTED:

The pace on the series is killing. You don't have the energy to mess around after a 12-hour day.

He added:

> I drop everything when I'm working – ladies included. It takes up all your life.

Within a month it was revealed that he had found some spare time and energy during the series to romance his *Dempsey and Makepeace* co-star, Glenys Barber.

In March 1985 *Dynasty* siren Pamela Sue Martin flew into London to promote her new film, denying that she was on the verge of a split from her second husband, millionaire Mañuel Rojas. It was later discovered she had already filed for divorce in Los Angeles citing 'irreconcilable differences'.

But you know these show-biz sex-lives:

> I've only been married three times and had three or four lovers. On today's market that's practically a virgin.
>
> *Shelley Winters, 1984*

> When I was 15 I said I would get married at 25. When I got to 25 I said it would be 35. Now I am 45 and still give myself another five years.
>
> *Kenny Lynch, May 1984*

> She out-Streisands Streisand. She's the new Judy Garland. What's more, she's got class.
>
> *Meshulam Riklis, husband of Pia Zadora*

> It has made things harder rather than easier for me. I had more work before I met Andrew

said Sarah Brightman on her marriage to superstar composer Andrew Lloyd-Webber. She also told how he had allowed her a part in his musical *Song and Dance*

Only after the most arduous audition.

Said husband Lloyd-Webber on his big-time Top Ten hit 'Pie Jesu' in April 1985:

The last thing in my mind was that it would have wide appeal.

Really, I'm just a frustrated cleaning lady and my home in Sheffield is the only place I can be myself.

Marti Caine, August 1984

In some ways I'm a lot like Vince. I like to flirt with women. Like Vince I value my freedom.

Paul Nicholas, on his screen role as Vince Pinner in 'Just Good Friends', 1984

I know I've said that in some ways I'm a lot like Vince, but the truth is I can't think of one similarity.

Paul Nicholas, on his screen role as Vince Pinner in 'Just Good Friends', 1985

You mustn't be seen having drinks. Even if it's a cup of tea or coffee. That's the viewers' licence money down the drain.

(An extremely thirsty) Cliff Michelmore on making BBC's 'Holiday' series, December 1984

But I still bet the crew got their full break.

I felt somehow I couldn't be happy without it. Maybe now I can accept the fact that I probably *am* an actor.

Ben Kingsley, pious on winning an Oscar for 'Gandhi', April 1984

Hall of Infamy

The following is a one-act play based on an incident in the life of Abraham Lincoln. The incident may or not be true, the point is I was tired when I wrote it.
Woody Allen

There's no way I will allow Brando to play the Don. He'll keep people out of the cinemas.
Paramount executive on 'The Godfather'

I'll never make another TV series after *Ivanhoe.*
Roger Moore, 1958

I'll never make another TV series after *Maverick.*
Roger Moore, 1959

I'll never make another TV series after *The Saint.*
Roger Moore, 1969. He went on to play opposite Tony Curtis in *The Persuaders.*

I'll never play Bond again.
Roger Moore after 'Moonraker', 1979 – emulating Sean Connery!

Roger will never play Bond again.
Moore's press agent Dennis Selinger after 'For Your Eyes Only', 1981

I have no plans to play Bond again.
Roger Moore after 'Octopussy', 1982. In 1985 he was back with another Bond movie, 'A View to a Kill'

Burt Reynolds is not a ladies' man at all. He's actually very shy.

Catherine Deneuve. So what about Dinah Shore, Judy Carne, Tammy Wynette, Chris Evert, Jill Clayburgh, Sally Field, Candice Bergen . . .?

Gone With The Wind is going to be the biggest flop in Hollywood history. I'm just glad it'll be Clark Gable who's falling flat on his face and not me.

Gary Cooper

I know when I married Peter Sellers I said I would be married for ever. And that was my intention and certainly what I wanted. Now I want Lou Adler and me to be together for ever and I think we will.

Britt Ekland. It lasted five months

I'll marry Paul McCartney this year.

Jane Asher, 1967

If I marry anyone it'll be Jane Asher.

Paul McCartney, 1967

My flirting days are over.

Susan George in September 1970, aged 19, before . . .

Just because a programme gets a zero rating doesn't mean a lot of people aren't watching it.

Channel-4 spokesman

There is going to be no axeing from TV-AM. No one is going to be kicked out and no one is going to walk the plank.

David Frost, March 1983

TV-AM is bloody rubbish, shabby, unprofessional, and garbage. I can't work there any more.

Michael Parkinson, April 20, 1983 (morning)

I am glad to be staying on. I was very happy with what Timothy Aitken said and I would like to be part of that progress.

Michael Parkinson, April 20, 1983 (afternoon)

THAT'S ENTERTAINMENT

4 POLITICS – BRITAIN

Said George Orwell: 'Political language – and with variations this is true of all political parties, from Conservatives to anarchists – is designed to make lies sound truthful and murder respectable, and to give an appearance of solidity to pure wind.'

The two issues which dominated British politics during the year were the economy and the miners' strike. More of MacGregor *v.* Scargill later – they merit a chapter all to themselves. But perhaps it would be a worthwhile investment (to use a catchy phrase) to look in this chapter at the man whose words brought together the twisted logic of both major issues: Chancellor Nigel Lawson.

If you can dig deep enough and work out what he said!

> MR LAWSON: Unlike most items of public expenditure, it is of a strictly temporary nature . . . And so, even in narrow financial terms, it represents a worthwhile investment for the nation.
> MR ROGERS: Did I understand the Chancellor to say that the miners' strike was a better investment for the nation?
> MR LAWSON: I certainly did not say that the strike was a good investment. (Hon. Members: 'He did.') What I did . . . (*Interruption.*)
> MR SPEAKER: Order!
> MR LAWSON: What I did say was that it was worthwhile for the Coal Board and for the nation to have the right to close uneconomic pits.
>
> *'The Times' parliamentary report, August 1, 1984*

Are you clear what he did say? No? Oh well. This should help, then.

I stand by everything that I said.

Nigel Lawson, August 2

Gee, thanks!

I don't regret the remark
said government minister Alan Clark in February, 1985, about his controversial reference to 'Bongo Bongo Land' – immediately adding, to clarify matters:
I don't remember if I said it or not.

Once again we can look back on a year of steady growth and low inflation.

Nigel Lawson, opening his Budget speech, March 1985

Pre-Ponting 1984 was the year Mrs Thatcher officially agreed that the Argentine cruiser, the *General Belgrano*, had been sailing *away from* and not towards the British task force when she was sunk. What's more, John Nott, the then Defence Secretary, had misled the Commons. Said the Prime Minister:

It must be borne in mind that Sir John's statement had to be prepared in fast-moving and sometimes confused circumstances.

Remember that one:
'I did not tell a lie, guv,
I was just making a
statement prepared in
fast-moving and
sometimes confused
circumstances.'

No. 10 Downing Street was demonstrably more to blame in February 1985 when a spokesman briefed reporters that:

> Mr Terry Waite's mission to Libya, which eventually resulted in the release of the four British detainees, was undertaken at the request of the Prime Minister.

According to the spokesman:

> Mrs Thatcher wrote to the Archbishop of Canterbury, Dr Runcie, suggesting that he send his personal representative to Tripoli after she had met relatives of the four at Downing Street on October 17 last year.

Dr Runcie issued a statement suggesting Downing Street was trying to steal the credit for Mr Waite's visit and pointing out that the Archbishop's first letter to Colonel Gaddafi had been sent *two and a half months earlier*, on August 1.

Hansard, the official parliamentary record which a year ago started getting censorious (replacing phrases like 'supercilious git' with something more innocuous) was at it again this year. During a debate on foreign aid Mr Timothy Raison, parliamentary under-secretary at the Foreign Office, rather foolhardily admitted government scissors had been at work. But his words:

> It may be a cut

came out happily for him in the official records as:

> It may be a calculation.

> It's just one of those things we don't generally do.
>
> *Mrs Glenys Kinnock after she and her husband had failed to join in the singing of 'God Save the Queen' at a pre-conference church service, Blackpool, September 1984*

Mr Kinnock sang at least part of the National Anthem. But he and Mrs Kinnock don't always say all the words.

Spokesman for Mr Neil Kinnock, Labour Party leader, the same morning

The highest courts in the land are the TUC and Labour Party conferences.

'London Labour Briefing', the gospel according to supporters of Ken Livingstone, December 1984

One of the most revealing of Forked Tongues came during the dockers' strike in September 1984. When, saying that most dockers wanted to work, the Port of London Authority organised a ballot, a Transport and General Workers Union spokesman fumed:

The ballot is a method of destroying the traditional means whereby our members are able to express their opinions in an open manner.

A ballot – yes – would bring

A distorted response that will not be acceptable to the union and its members as a true indication of the wishes of the majority.

But you know elections:

We got a really good consensus during the last election. Consensus behind my convictions.

Margaret Thatcher, May 1984

Hall of Infamy

There have been improvements in security at the palace over the past 18 months.

Viscount Whitelaw (Deputy Conservative Party Leader, Leader of the House of Lords, former Home Secretary, Minister with Special Responsibility for the Avoidance of Banana Skins) is one of Britain's most endearing political figures. The reason – his verbal gaffes. Among them . . .

They are going round the country stirring up complacency.

On Labour ministers, 1974

We are examining alternative anomalies.

I don't blame anyone, except, perhaps, all of us.

I have the thermometer in my mouth and I am listening to it all the time.

I will have a little whisky.

On being offered a drink by a local worker

When I say I would like a little whisky, I mean I would like a large one, thank you very much.

Explaining subsequent tetchiness to local party worker

The Archbishop of Canterbury is a very religious man.

Of Dr Robert Runcie, October 1984

The resounding majority we were given in last May's election showed clearly that we have the country's support for a consistent strategy.

March 1984. Oops! The election had been in June

I have always thought it a great mistake ever to prejudge the past.

As Secretary for Ulster, pronouncing on IRA parades

'WILLYISMS'

5 POLITICS – INTERNATIONAL

After American denials of 'intervention' in Grenada and Soviet insistence that they did not shoot down Korean Airlines Flight 007, it might have been a quiet year for Forked Tongues internationally . . . if it hadn't been for that shooting outside the Libyan People's Bureau, and the American presidential election:

> I know we're going to win this. I know we're going to be elected. That's what the American people want.
>
> *Walter Mondale, May 1984*

> Hands that once picked cotton on Tuesday will pick a President. The waking of a sleeping giant has been a long time coming, but our time has come.
>
> *Reverend Jesse Jackson, a little prematurely, April 1, 1984*

In April 1984 *Pravda*'s view of the shooting of WPC Fletcher outside the Libyan People's Bureau in St James's Square was that it was 'provocation' by Britain.

> The gunfire started outside the building . . .

Asserted the Soviets:

> Britain tried to violate the Libyans' diplomatic immunity under the muscles of specially trained police units and army commandos.

After the murder of WPC Yvonne Fletcher came the news from Libya:

> The British police were to blame. The people inside the People's Bureau had a right to defend themselves when they found they were under attack by helicopters and police forces.
>
> *Libyan leader Colonel Muammar Gaddafi, April 1984*

Said an Iraqi official after air strikes were unleashed on four Iranian towns in March 1985,

But it is the only language the Iranians understand.

They got it wrong in 1948 and they've got it wrong again this time.

Walter Mondale on opinion polls, November 1984

Talking of underestimating language,

A good meeting

was the official word on the talks in November 1984, between US Secretary of State, George Shultz and Soviet Premier Nikolai Tikhonov in New Delhi. Actually Mr Secretary Shultz had given the Soviet premier a severe talking-to about Russian accusations that the CIA had been involved in the murder of Mrs Indira Gandhi. Another spokesman was more honest; he admitted:

There was a lot of shouting.

The death of Soviet defence minister Marshal Ustinov (did you notice how he was the most decorated and bemedalled military man in history – yet was never a serving soldier, spending his entire life behind a desk ordering arms?) exposed a whole farrago of Forked Tongues in the Kremlin, many of which were to be repeated during the illness of President Chernenko.

When Marshal Ustinov lay on his death-bed in December 1984, the Kremlin put out its usual medical smokescreen to explain his public absence. In November, when he failed to turn up at the annual military parade in Red Square, another member of the Politburo, Viktor Grishin, declared earnestly:

He has a sore throat.

You may recall that in August 1983 Soviet leader Yuri Andropov disappeared from public view, not to be seen again until after his death six months later. During that time the Kremlin maintained that he was fit, well and fulfilling all his State functions:

> He is carrying out his duties as General Secretary of the Central Committee and Chairman of the Praesidium of the Supreme Soviet.
>
> *September 1983*

> He is dealing extensively with party and state business.
>
> *Kremlin comment on Yuri Andropov's prolonged absence, September 1983*

When, finally, Andropov failed to show up at the annual parade in Red Square, the Kremlin's chief spokesman, Leonid Zamyatin declared:

> Mr Andropov was unable to attend today's parade because of a cold.
>
> *November 1983*

As one Western Kremlinologist joked, 'Colds in the Soviet Union do tend to be fatal.'

> I never did wear make-up. I didn't even wear it when I was in pictures.
>
> *Ronald Reagan on the election trail, October 1984*

Unfortunately, not only did a studio hand come forward and tell how he'd made up the President for an episode of *Wagon Train*, in his biography *Where's the Rest of Me?* Reagan had told how he had been in the make-up room before his first screen test.

In public Forked Tongues, the French have a style of their own. When, in August 1984, the French freighter *Mont Louis* sank in the Channel carrying an unidentified cargo, its owners said:

The ship was carrying medical supplies.

It transpired that the *Mont Louis* had been ferrying 450 tonnes of radioactive gas; a full nuclear alert followed.

I've met half the town. They'll all vote twice, so that's everyone.

Canadian Conservative leader Brian Mulroney on the stump, August 1984

Asked at a NATO briefing in March 1985 why the Americans had asked Australia and not the recalcitrant New Zealand to join a research programme into strategic defence systems, US Defense Secretary Caspar Weinberger replied: 'We didn't have the address.'

And so to electoral matters. The Sultan of Brunei said in March 1984, on why his country had had no elections for 22 years:

People competed with each other and chaos resulted.

When Reagan was finally declared the victor, the re-elected President lost no time in showing us why he had been dubbed 'the great communicator'. He declared:

We come together!

meaning . . . wait a moment, just what *does* it mean?

This is the end of nothing and the beginning of everything!

Pardon? Well, at least there can be no doubt of what the oldest President in US history meant when he told the world:

From now on, it's shake, rattle and roll!

6 DES. RES.? – FIFTY AMAZING EXAMPLES OF BLUFF AND BLARNEY FROM ESTATE AGENTS' HAND-OUTS

A couple of years ago, looking for a home in North London, we were amazed to discover that every property not in one of the prime areas was designated 'Hampstead borders', 'Highgate borders', or, getting the best of both worlds, 'Hampstead/Highgate borders'. Every house in North London, it seemed, 'bordered' on fashionable Hampstead or Highgate – except for a few on the 'borders' of trendy Islington.

The estate agents excelled themselves throughout. Our particular favourites were:

- *leafy outlook* – a gigantic tree – plonk in front of all the back windows blocked out all the light; and
- *views over Highgate Woods . . .*

The latter was, up to a point, quite accurate. The views *were* over Highgate Woods – since all you could see if you peered beyond the houses opposite was sky (if you climbed on to the dressing table or wore stilts you could just see the tops of three trees in the distance).

What they say	**What they mean**
charming	completely unmodernised; needs £5000 spent on it
residence of character	dilapidated
desirable	average
stunning/imposing	ugly
character residence	tumbled down
scope for improvement	wet rot, dry rot, woodworm
suit collector	hideous, tasteless decor

What they say	What they mean
adorable/bijou/compact/ ideal bachelor pad	midget-sized
superb/immaculate	recently fumigated
airy	ill-fitting windows
full of atmosphere	no damp course, poor drains
must be viewed internally	outside looks like a public lavatory
interesting/unusual	homemade
townhouse	recently built terrace
starter home	so small that you'll want to move within six months
garden flat	cellar; pot plants outside
1/2 reception rooms	1 lounge, 1 closet
2/3 bedrooms	2 bedrooms, 1 cupboard
music room	alcove
third bedroom	boxroom
library/study	cloakroom
wine cellar	coal cellar
luxuriously appointed	imitation gold bath taps and door handles
substantially modernised	window frames rotten, roof leaks

What they say	What they mean
luxury development	new houses, built a yard apart, with tiny gardens
individually designed/unique	last psychopathic owner let rip with Black and Decker
low outgoings	tiny
prestige	overpriced
superior	on a hill
outstanding	hideous extension
unspoilable tranquillity	subsidence nearby
prime location	sky-high rates bill
unusual	no chance of a mortgage
town garden	minuscule plot
mature garden	overgrown plot
large patio	back yard
convenient for shops, schools	you'll need a car
convenient for motorway	M6 at end of garden
country views	backs on to pig farm
near picturesque mediaeval village	picturesque mediaeval village 15 minutes' drive away
period property	about to fall down
needs attention	falling down

What they say	What they mean
offers potential	has fallen down
quiet neighbourhood	backs on to cemetery
popular choice	working-class area
highly recommended	can't sell fast enough
under new instructions/ realistically priced	reduced and on the books of every estate agent in town
offers considered	will do anything to sell
must be seen	nothing to be said for it – defies even the estate agent's powers of description!
evokes emotional response	we hope for a lunatic buyer

7 UNTRUTH WILL OUT

A halber emez iz a gantzer lign (a half truth is a whole lie).
Yiddish proverb

A lie can travel round the world while the truth is putting on its boots.
Mark Twain

Some Forked Tongues do not start as premeditated lies. It's just that, in the fullness of time, all is naturally, often embarrassingly – and sometimes hilariously – revealed. Here are some cases this year when the truth, most definitely, did out:

The choice of Mrs Ferraro as vice-presidential candidate has turned the election from a landslide for President Reagan into a horse race.
Louis Harris, pollster, August 1984

A one-horse race?

Never again. It was the most terrifying experience of my life.
Round-the-world sailsman Chay Blyth from a hospital bed in Chile after 21 hours adrift off Cape Horn in a capsized trimaran, November 1984

A month later he was back on board declaring:
It'll take more than a capsize to keep Blyth from the water.

And . . .

> I believe that if you're thrown from a horse you get straight back on and set off at a gallop.

> I am convinced that for Britain, at least, George Orwell was wrong. 1984 will be a year of hope and a year of liberty.
>
> *Margaret Thatcher, New Year's message, December 31, 1983*

Well, not quite. Remember Brighton . . . static unemployment . . . the emasculation of the metropolitan councils.

> The prospect for jobs is becoming brighter. We have shown what can be done. But this is only the beginning of a revival of Britain.
>
> *Margaret Thatcher, New Year's message, December 31, 1983*

Now I know she was talking through her hat.

> A sum of 250 million rupees has been invested in this unit. The factory is not a small stone which can be shifted elsewhere. There is no danger to Bhopal, nor will there be.
>
> *Tarasingh Viyogi, Bhopal's Labour Minister, 1982, on the Union Carbide plant, an accident in which, in November 1984, caused one of the world's worst tragedies*

I'm going to be the first Vice-President to enjoy being a woman.

Geraldine Ferraro, July 1984

Some helpful predictions were on a more personal level:

He'll come home.

Mrs Susan Sangster, November 1984, on her straying husband's departure with leggy blonde Mrs Susan Lilley.

A month later, she announced she was seeking separation or divorce.

I never expected Rod to cheat. I expected the opposite because he was so adamant about how important it was to be faithful.

Alana Stewart, July 1984

I've never had the slightest fantasy about anyone else. I'm just not interested. Before, it was morality that stopped me experimenting. Now it's God. And feeling this has absolutely welded John and me together.

Cristina Ferrare, wife of disgraced car boss, John De Lorean, July 1984.

Unfortunately God did not stop them being wrenched asunder immediately after his trial for cocaine smuggling (he was cleared).

1984 was the year Julie Walters revealed that, when she had told her mother she was going to be an actress, she got the encouraging reply:

You'll be in the gutter before you're 20.

I will not be indicted.

US Labor Secretary Raymond Donovan, October 1984, up before the New York State Supreme Court on grand-larceny and fraud charges.

Shortly afterwards, Donovan became the first US cabinet minister ever to be indicted. He later resigned.

> My husband is not suffering from brain damage. He's had doctor's tests and come out completely healthy.
>
> *Mrs Veronica Ali, July 1984.*

Three months later, the former world champion was found to be suffering from an illness with effects similar to those of Parkinson's Disease.

> THE POLLS ARE WRONG
>
> *Walter Mondale campaign sticker*

Oh no, they weren't.

Hall of Infamy

Soviet political officials are perfectly agreed with me that a boycott is an incorrect political tool.

Peter Ueberroth, President of the Los Angeles Olympic Organising Committee, August 1983

Tony Benn doesn't stand a snowball's chance in hell.

Liberal Party spokesman, January 1984, on the ex-MP's chances in the Chesterfield by-election. Benn was an easy winner

Princess Di can expect five more children. The next, a girl, will be born next year.

Russell Grant, the 'inflatable astrologer', 'Sunday People', June 1983, on the forthcoming Prince Harry

I am off to a sprinter's start in a marathon.

Senator Alan Cranston, Democratic Party challenger, January 1983

I have decided to quit as a full-time soccer manager four years from now. That statement is not meant to shock people, to stir them up or to frighten them. It is a fact.

Brian Clough, November 1978

The good news is beginning to roll in.

Senator John Glenn, on the start of his campaign, June 1983

It's not going to fail. It's going to be very successful.

John De Lorean, October 1978, on his Northern Ireland car plant

We will be here for ever now.

General Oswaldo Garcia, Argentine commander on the Falklands

Comprehensive schools will have gone out in 10 or 15 years' time.

Margaret Thatcher, 1970

Both Elizabeth and I will retire from acting within the next two years.

Richard Burton, 1968

He is OK in the West and South . . . a little shaky in the Northeast.

Senator Paul Laxalt, October 1983, predicting a close race for Reagan in 1984

JUMPING THE GUN

8 ROCK AND POP

> Being in a pop group is the biggest bluff of all time. It's the biggest con going. It's a complete fantasy world. A great concert is when the fans don't hear a note for the screaming.
>
> *Simon Le Bon of Duran Duran*

Yes, here is another world in which things are not all that they might seem . . .

Remember how Frankie Goes to Hollywood blitzed into the charts in 1984 amid some sensationally bad (i.e., good – and money-spinning) publicity, notably a BBC ban of one of their records and the claim that all the band were gay? In June 1984 the deception couldn't be sustained any more. It was revealed, heaven forbid, that there were *heterosexuals* in the group (publicity man throws himself through ninth-floor window).

> In fact it's only Holly Johnson and I who are gay.
>
> *Frankie band member Paul Rutherford, June 1984*

Talk about a ruined image!

> We're playing to full houses and there's pandemonium wherever we go.
>
> *Said Boy George of Culture Club as his US tour got under way in November 1984*

How was it, then, that a 19,000 seat stadium in Dallas was only half-full and a New York concert was cancelled, it is rumoured, by poor ticket sales? Said George:

> If there are empty spaces it's only because we don't copy other groups by selling seats behind the stage.
>
> *November 1984*

Come off it George! If you sold seats behind the stage, there'd be vast empty spaces up front.

Culture Club returned to Britain to more mysteriously cancelled tour dates and what was described as 'a lukewarm reception' before just 8,000 fans in Birmingham, with 'just a few screams'. A new release *The Medal Song* failed to make the Top 30, and the hottest name in pop of a year ago seemed to be suddenly out of fashion. Boy George himself was said to be 'in a sulk' after failing to get a single nomination at a big record awards shindig.

Francis Rossi of Status Quo told an interviewer in January 1984:

> Just because the band is older, why should we stop when we are having such a good time? I shall never be tired of touring. I shall probably be like Keith Richard and play until I drop.

All we appear to have talked about for two years is our sex-lives – actually we made it all up.
Wham! star George Michael, December 1984

Within weeks it was announced the group would play their last tour in the summer of that same year. But Rossi does seem to change his mind. In February 1984 he told David Hancock of the *Sun*:

> I don't think it's fair to bring children into the world. Everything seems to be heading to a great big bang.

In August he celebrated the birth of his 7lb 10oz baby girl with long-standing girlfriend Liz Gernon.

Andy Ridgeley of Wham! laid elaborate plans in the summer of 1984 to cover-up a £2,000 nose-job. He told people how he needed treatment for his face after being hit with a champagne bucket at a party in a fight over a girl . . . He said later:

> I've had a nose job and we dreamed up the idea of a fight as a cover. We thought we'd got away with it.

Two of the great song-writing teams there . . . Lennon and McCartney and Ivor Novello.

Jimmy Savile, BBC Radio 1, July 1984

Some Forked Tongues in the pop world are not so much fibs or inaccuracies as just . . . well, curios:

I'm not pretending to be anyone – I'm just being myself.

Marilyn, alias Peter Robinson, June 1984

It's a bit like a *ménage à trois*, except that I don't go to bed with Joe.

Alannah Currie of the Thompson Twins on her relationship with fellow band members Tom Bailey and Joe Leeway, December 1984

There were so many famous DJs at the party that it's surprising any radio station stayed on the air. Among the big names were . . . John Sachs, and Richard Allinson.

John Blake, 'Daily Mirror', January 1985

Who? Big names did he say? I suppose Richard Allinson is a big name in a way – it does have 15 letters.

I'm doing geography and metalwork at sixth-form college, and if I don't make it to be a roadie for Def Leppard I'm going to be a doctor: one, because you can look up girls' jumpers; two, they make so much they can go to the Reading three-day festival and the one at Castle Donington, every year.

'Headbanger' Smudge Midgely, 18, quoted in the 'Observer' colour magazine, February 1985

Harriet Vidal, spokeswoman for sultry American pop idol Prince, told us in February 1985 why he refused to join the American charity famine-appeal record, 'We Are the World':

It is not the kind of thing that he does. It isn't that he didn't want to give. That's all he does – give, give, give.

Sometimes the stars, well, do stretch the imagination a bit.

We are five ordinary lads from Liverpool. We tell it like it is and people can see that.
Paul Rutherford of Frankie Goes to Hollywood, June 1984

I don't have any friends at the local station yet, but no doubt I'll be making some soon.
David Emanuel, alias 'Smiley Culture', after his irreverent hit single 'Police Officer', January 1985

Three O levels and a lot of mouth – that's worth about £70,000 a year!
Disc jockey Steve Wright, December 1984

Somebody asked me what I thought of Wham! and I didn't know what Wham! was – I thought it was a comic.
Adam Ant, on his return from America, November 1984

I know why they go through my cases – it's to see what colour my smalls are.
Boy George on Customs men, October 1984

My ambition? To star in *Emmerdale Farm.*
Josie Warden of the outrageous punk group Vicious Pink, January 1985

It takes about four minutes to write a three-minute song.
Hugh Cornwell of The Stranglers

It's been said that we could go on stage and fart and it wouldn't make any difference.
Andy Taylor of Duran Duran, May 1984

I became an absolute lunatic. I blew a fortune and now I'm broke. Okay, I'm still a millionaire, but I'm a lot poorer than I was.
Connie Francis, singer, November 1984

Hall of Infamy

Honestly, I wasn't expecting a hit. When we were in London three weeks ago the main thing I wanted to do was meet Jimmy Savile.

Sonny Bono, 1965

I hate violence, nastiness, and ignorance. I hate that kind of yob mentality.

Punk pioneer Johnny Rotten

I enjoy writing and performing rock, but not listening to it.

Sting, January 1984

Q. How did you feel about being booed at your concert at Forest Hills?
A. I thought it was great, I really did. If I said anything else I'd be a liar.

Bob Dylan

We are not getting divorced, nor are we taking any steps to dissolve our marriage. There are no disagreements between us about our child or any other subject.

Joint statement by Mick and Bianca Jagger, New York, 1978

My favourite Abba song is 'Fernando'.

Agnetha Faltskog, 'The Late Late Breakfast Show', BBC TV, November 6, 1982

If I had to choose a favourite Abba record it would be 'The Winner Takes All'

Agnetha Faltskog, 'Mail on Sunday', November 7, 1982

You have to do things in this world to make people sit up. It sounds a bit biblical, but I think I'm on a mission.

Ozzy Osbourne, after memorable performance when he bit off the head of a live bat on stage

God, those Rolling Stones are horrible. They're all greasy and spotty.

Marianne Faithfull, before she went on to become Mick Jagger's first superstar girlfriend

Apart from his little idiosyncracies, he comes across as a regular sort of chap.

Pauline McLeod, 'Daily Mirror', on Boy George

She died the day I was born. I'm her reincarnation.

'Marilyn', on Marilyn Monroe

Duran *who*? I've never heard of them.

Eric Burdon, December 1983

You think I look suntanned?

Grace Kennedy, arriving back from honeymoon, March 1982

9 ROYALTY

As *Forked Tongues* proved, even the loftiest in the land sometimes don't tell the whole truth. In return, though, they too can find themselves the subjects of 'factual inaccuracies'.

One of the blackest lies told about the Royal Family during the year came during a cheap publicity stunt for a West End night club called 'Shaftesburys'. Manager Gerry Summers told how, in December 1984, Prince Andrew had been enjoying candlelight dinners with a young raven-haired temptress called Vicki Macdonald. Gushed Summers, according to one report:

> They are very much in love.

The story was eagerly regurgitated by Sunday tabloids under headlines like:

> VICKI'S 'PARTY FUN WITH ANDREW'
>
> *'Sunday Mirror', December 9, 1984*

She was rather more coy, saying merely:

> I am a fast lady. I am a night person.

Which only excited some gullible scandal-sheets all the more.

Surprisingly enough, during the time that the happy couple were supposed to have been enjoying their *tête-à-têtes*, Prince Andrew had been either at Balmoral or on a tour of duty with HMS *Brazen*, in his capacity as a Royal Navy helicopter pilot. In fact, he had never met her.

Also beastly to a member of the Royal Family during the year was 6ft 4in Canadian politician James Snow. During a tour which had its ups and downs – not least when one newspaper described Her Majesty as 'dowdy' – Mr Snow received a frosty reaction from the Queen when he repeatedly touched her in the 'small of the back' during the opening ceremony of a new highway at Amherstview, in

October 1984. Onlookers said the Queen was 'visibly annoyed, stony-faced and grim' as the touchy Mr Snow – nicknamed 'Friendly' – 'gave her a hand'. He explained himself thus:

> It's possible I may have touched her by accident. It was purely to help. I'm the last person in the world to offend the Queen. I'm just a hick from the sticks who likes to be friendly.

But the Royal Family themselves aren't always blameless. Royal denial of the year came from Major John Griffin, equerry to Princess Margaret. After she had had a small lung operation at London's Brompton Hospital in January, Major Griffin spent the day of January 13, 1985, on the telephone to newspapermen saying:

> The Princess will definitely not be leaving hospital today.

The Princess left hospital later that day.

> It was an accident. The Prince's hand slipped on the trigger.
>
> *John Hulton, British Vice-Consul in Los Angeles, April 1984, after Prince Andrew had childishly sprayed photographers with paint. Andrew was seen to laugh and remarked: 'I enjoyed that.' Compensation was later paid.*

In April 1985, Prince Charles and Princess Diana unexpectedly cancelled a mass with the Pope during their Italian tour. On the spot, assistant Buckingham Palace press secretary Victor Chapman said there 'wasn't time'. He added: 'It was a logistical rather than an ecumenical decision.'

But the rug was pulled from under Mr Chapman's feet back at the Palace itself with an admission that it was thought the mass might be 'inappropriate' for a future head of the Church of England, and might embarrass the Queen. Said Palace official Mr John Haslam:

> Prince Charles took advice from a lot of sources. The final choice was taken by the Prince himself.

Royal slip of the year came from the Princess of Wales during the film of Prince Harry's christening shown as part of the Queen's Christmas 1984 TV broadcast. Explaining to Prince William how generations of Royals had been baptized in the gown his baby brother wore, the Princess said:

> Great Granny was christened in it. Yes!

Prince Charles with a quizzical expression, but obviously not wanting to start a family row on camera, repeated:

> Great Granny was christened in it.

Great Granny – the Queen Mother – married *into* the Royal Family, of course, and so was not baptized in the robe. A Buckingham Palace spokesman pronounced:

> Great Granny's husband was christened in it. Great Granny wasn't.

> If people in England think it's cold, they should be here in Gstaad.
>
> *Princess Michael, January 1985*

Chance would be a fine thing!

King Hussein of Jordan left the Cleveland Clinic in

February 1984 after a series of tests for what were described as
Ulcers.

An indiscreet State Department source said:
His doctors thought ulcers sounded more kingly than haemorrhoids.

I'm a lonely recluse who only makes friends when they come along.
Prince Andrew, July 1984

We've nearly got a polo team.
Prince Charles on the birth of his second son, Harry

The Royals are ever so ordinary, of course. In August 1984 Prince Charles worked for 12 hours on a Somerset farm as a labourer. A farm-hand said:
He just mucked in.

10 THE MINERS' STRIKE

Nowhere did Forked Tongues proliferate during the year so much as in the region of the miners' strike. From disputed back-to-work statistics to the prevalence – or absence – of picket-line violence, here was perfect proof that the Big Lie was alive . . . and kicking.

A Short Sharp Strike

> Sources in the CEGB have verified that there are only eight to nine weeks' supply of coal left for the power stations at the present rate of burn.
>
> *Arthur Scargill, March 30, 1984*

Wrong.

> Emergency measures containing power cuts on a rota basis will be presented to parliament shortly. The cuts will be introduced either late in August or early in September.
>
> *Arthur Scargill, June 27, 1984*

Wrong.

> We are on our way to an historic victory.
>
> *Arthur Scargill, 'Sunday Telegraph', July 1984*

And . . . wrong.

> We will stop the importation of coal and we will stop the transportation of coal.
>
> *NUM Vice-President Mick McGahey, March 1984*

But other unions – including those in Poland – didn't support them.

ONLY THE TUC CAN GET THE MINERS BACK
Leading article, 'Daily Mirror', July 1984

If we have to stay out until November or December, we will beat the Coal Board and this Government.
Arthur Scargill, May 1984

Scargillisms

The coal stocks are like my hairstyle – a lot round the sides but nothing in the middle.
June 1984

I am a reasonable man who always tries to avoid trouble.
Denying obstruction charges, December 1984

I think people will react to our meeting in a positive way.
On evening visit to the Soviet Embassy to ask for assistance, November 1984

MacGregorisms

I am not combative.
'Daily Express', July 1984

. . . the fiction of people going down and hazarding themselves underground is some kind of unnecessary nonsense.
'Daily Express', July 1984

The last thing we wish to see is the NUM wrenched apart.
Ian MacGregor Press conference, July 1984

Governmentisms

I really do not see any role for government intervention.
Margaret Thatcher, interview with George Gale, June 1984. She was later to boast in Kuala Lumpur about how she had 'seen off' the miners

There is no question of 'beating the miners'.
David Hunt, Junior Energy Minister, January 1985

Strange that, a couple of weeks later, another government minister, Mr John Butcher, should be saying:

The end of the miners' strike will not represent victory for the government – it will be a victory for the country.
February 1985

On Violence

Hundreds of people have been arrested, hundreds beaten up and crippled. Britain is rapidly becoming a police state under Mrs Thatcher's government.
Ray Buckton, left-wing ASLEF boss in the Soviet labour magazine, 'Trud', March 1984

The picketing has, despite press suggestions, been peaceful.
TUC statement, March 1984

Mass picketing is not intimidation.
Labour Party General Secretary Jim Mortimer, March 1984

I've never been on a picket line without police violence.
Scottish NUM President Mick McGahey, BBC TV News, June 1984

If you ask me they've done him a favour. He'll get the insurance.

Upton, Pontefract, NUM spokesman on the burning-down of the home of a working miner, ITN News, November 1984

On Democracy

I am not contemplating any action because there seems to be a division of opinion which makes it unwise for the national officers to intervene. The response from the areas highlights the division in the NUM at this time. By contrast, the unanimous resolution carried by the Executive on March 8 was very clear.

Peter Heathfield, NUM General Secretary, March 1984, on why there was no ballot

In other words, the executive decides, the members must follow. Mr Heathfield called attempts by moderates to force a vote:

A conspiracy by right-wingers to defeat the will of the majority.

March 1984

I shall have to rule out of order a resolution which need not be put.

Arthur Scargill on South Derbyshire NUM leader Ken Toon's support for a ballot, 'Sunday Times', April 1984

We cannot afford to wind down the action and bring pickets home for an exercise in democracy.

Ian Isaac, a member of the South Wales NUM executive, April 1984

Coal Board Knickers-in-a-Twist Time

The chairman has decided that in view of the sensational developments over the weekend [the Libyan connection] which have changed the whole situation, all Mr Eaton's appointments with the press will not now go ahead.

Coal Board statement, October 29, on behalf of Chairman Ian MacGregor on why the new head of publicity was no longer talking

I have cancelled my press conference in the light of the forthcoming talks.

Michael Eaton, October 29 – on why he was no longer talking

But There's a Lighter Side:

We are not using the word pickets. Our members are lobbying.

South Wales NUM President Emlyn Williams, March 1984

When miners face miners, they are always friends.

South Wales NUM branch official Tyrone O'Sullivan, March 1984

We don't believe this strike should have started in the first place.

Arthur Scargill, ITN News, January 1985

11 EIGHTEEN ROMANTIC AND BELIEVABLE ALIBIS FOR NOT TURNING UP ON TIME FOR A DATE

She says	He shouldn't think . . .
I was searching through some tour brochures for a very special holiday for the two of us . . .	Costs me a mint, two single rooms, *and* she'll want to bring mum, dad, brother and the cocker spaniel.
I had to go to the building society to see about a *joint* account.	Crikes. Not content with spending her money and her dad's money, she wants to get at mine too.
I was trying to look my best for you, but Dad and Simon were in the bathroom all the time and I couldn't get ready in time . . .	Come off it. Not during the 'World Snooker Championships'.
I heard a busker singing your favourite tune – it was so moving, I just had to stop and listen . . .	*Singing* Ravel's Bolero?
I was searching for an eye shadow to match your beautiful bright blue eyes.	They're brown.
It took me ages to choose your Valentine. But when you see it, it's the best ever.	But Valentine's Day isn't for another eight months.
I was so busy thinking about you I went on past my train stop.	But ours is the last station on the line.

She says	**He shouldn't think . . .**
There was a film on with Robert de Niro. I had to watch it to the end because he's *so like you*.	Except that I could give him a year or two and he could give me a million or two.
I was engrossed in a book showing what energetic things we could get up to together when we were all alone.	Not *another* keep-fit manual.
I couldn't remember whether you said 6 p.m. or 6.30 p.m., so I split the difference and came at 6.45 p.m.	With logic like that, you should go into politics.

He says	**She shouldn't think . . .**
I was on the 'phone longer than I thought making arrangements for a very special occasion for the two of us . . .	Not trying to get tickets for Arsenal *v.* Manchester United *again* . . .
I was hunting for a very special piece of jewellery . . .	*Another* fully digitised automatic Barry Sheene action-man scuba-dive-proof wrist-alarm watch.

He says	She shouldn't think . . .
I've just heard some very sad news from Australia. It took me a while to pull myself together.	Another Test Match flop.
I was leafing through the holiday brochures . . . I was carried away by the description of this Mediterranean idyll . . .	So you're going on another singles holiday next year, you rat!
I was just cleaning the car passenger-seat to make sure you don't dirty your coat.	Looking for damning evidence like blonde hairs and hairgrips, more like.
I've been learning off by heart the love-poem I'm going to dedicate to you at the end of what I know will be the most wonderful, enchanting evening ever . . .	He's going to try to get me drunk.
I was readying the oysters and champagne for a late-night supper back at my place . . .	Presumptuous so-and-so.
I wanted to bring flowers but the shop was shut and I had to drive to the florist's home and drive him back to the premises. I got the	

He says

flowers, but getting out of the car the door slammed unexpectedly and half the blooms disintegrated. That wouldn't have been too bad if the rest hadn't been eaten by a rampaging escaped circus elephant when I was hit by lightning and tripped over the foot of a man selling Mexican jumping beans outside the Cathedral . . .

The cab driver gave me a £20 note in my change by mistake . . . I had to get in another taxi and chase after him to give him his money back . . .

She shouldn't think . . .

Boy, can he spin a yarn.

A cabbie giving a £20 note by mistake – that's the dumbest lie I've ever heard!!!

12 MONSTERS, WHOPPERS – CAN YOU BELIEVE THEM?

In *The Decay of Lying* Oscar Wilde feared for the future of the liar and his art as twentieth-century realism swamped human inventiveness. But, if he returned today, he would surely find 'the telling of beautiful untrue things' restored to its former glory.

To me it was like having a glass of wine.

Mafia hit-man Ray Ferrito on how it felt to kill a rival Irish gangster in Cleveland, Ohio, as told to ITV's 'Crime Inc.', August 1984

Plans existed to drug and kidnap Soviet athletes and force them to defect.

Marat Gramov, president of the Soviet Olympic committee, on why Russia wouldn't be at Los Angeles, May 1984

I'm on your side.

Union Carbide Chairman Warren Anderson calling for tighter federal regulation on the chemical industry after the Bhopal explosion, December 1984

Representative Henry Waxman, Chairman of the House Subcommittee on Health and Environment, asked why then, had Union Carbide opposed new safety regulations in the past?

I am going to see the consultant on Monday and I'm likely to be in hospital for the rest of the week.

Lancashire miners' leader Sid Vincent to NUM area agent Stan Horsfield as he took off for a winter break in Tenerife with a female companion, December 1984

I have got five dollars for each of you.

'Death Wish' gunman Hugo Goetz, 37, to four assumed muggers on the New York subway as he pulled out a silver pistol and shot each one, December 1984

The case of Clive Ponting, the senior Ministry of Defence civil servant who leaked secret files on the sinking of the Argentine cruiser, the *General Belgrano*, brought a whole farrago of Forked Tongues . . . even from Ponting himself:

The Old Bailey heard in January 1985 how he had told police:

> Good God, you don't suspect me? I can see there is a strong circumstantial case against me, but honestly I did not do it.

He later changed his story somewhat.

And then there was Ian Smith, former white ruler of Rhodesia (now Zimbabwe), who explained colleague Desmond Chalmers' derogatory remarks in November 1984 to a Canadian newspaper about 'kaffirs' with the ingenious statement:

> The term 'kaffir' is racially neutral. Its dictionary meaning is that of 'non-believer in God'.

He later agreed that, yes, 'Kaffirs' *was* a racial slur.

By the end of 1984 it became clear that the Marxist Ethiopian government was doing little to prevent the deaths of thousands if not millions in that country from starvation and disease – despite vigorous attempts by international relief agencies. Strange, then, that in March 1983 Mr Wilfred Agnes, Canadian Ambassador to Nairobi, should have said:

> The Ethiopian Government has, in my experience, a more than reasonable record in handling aid.

Allegations that grain shipments were being 'misappropriated' were investigated by the European Economic Community. The EEC's Commissioner for Development Policy, Mr Adgard Pisani, in April 1983 said:

> I am satisfied the aid has been used correctly and with efficiency.

Try telling that to the people of Tigre Province. Other shipments were being diverted even before leaving their country of origin:

> DIPLOMATIC BAGGAGE – Catering Equipment.
>
> *Large-lettered lie on the crate shipping a drugged Mr Umaro Dikko back to Nigeria, July 1984*

> We are not lunatics but people who behave in a responsible way.
>
> *Animal-rights activists who caused panic with their poisoned Mars Bar scare, November 1984*

Did they say *responsible*? Of course. Like the people who desecrated the grave of the Duke of Beaufort in December 1984 (they had wanted to make off with his skull), and then turned up at hunts with placards reading 'Dig deeper for the Duke.' Actually, it's all a question of responsibility.

> The Government is directly responsible for the trouble in the coalfields.
>
> *Gerald Kaufman, shadow Home Secretary, April 1984*

Directly responsible? Come off it.

> We are not selling to a single bidder.
>
> *Sir Alex Jarratt, Chairman of Reed International, June 1984, on the sale of Mirror Group Newspapers*

Sir Alex said later he had sold the group to Robert Maxwell for £113 million because that was 'almost twice' as much as he could have raised by offering shares to a wide spread of investors.

My integrity is unimpugned.

Dr Brian Richards, June 1984, after receiving a four-year sentence in California for conspiracy to murder his partner

The IRA action in Brighton was an inevitable result of the British occupation of the six counties.

Gerry Adams, President of Sinn Fein, October 1984

Who is Sid Vincent? I am Jim Smith from Gloucestershire.

First words of Lancashire miners' leader Sid Vincent after being trailed by reporters to Tenerife, December 1984

Hall of Infamy

You will be home before the leaves have fallen from the trees.

Kaiser Wilhelm to German troops, August 1914

Gaiety is the most outstanding feature of the Soviet Union.

Joseph Stalin, 1935

We only wish to pursue our work with honour and peace!

Joseph Goebbels

Well, he seemed such a nice old gentleman, I thought I would give him my autograph as a souvenir.

Adolf Hitler on the worthless Munich 'piece of paper for peace' obtained by Neville Chamberlain, 1938

We want war with no nation.

Yoshuke Matsuoka, Japanese Foreign Minister 1940–41

There are no permanent enemies in politics.

Idi Amin. True for him – he killed his

I want to see peace, prosperity and happiness in my country, and I think the way we are going about it is the best way.

Joe Cahill, leader of the Provisional IRA, on his campaign of bombings and murder, October 1971

We do not wish to impose a Communist regime in Saigon. What we want is the establishment of a three-segment government of national concord.

Le Duc Tho, Hanoï's chief negotiator at Paris, 1972

Our coming to our neighbour – at his urgent request – is not aggression or intervention, as ill intentioned slanderers try to prove. The only task before the Soviet military contingent is to help Afghanistan repel the threat from outside.

'Red Star', Soviet army newspaper

Argentina had no choice but to take over the Malvinas.

Argentine governmental spokesman after the Franks report, January 1983

BLACK LIES OF HISTORY

13 WHITE LIES – AND A SLIGHT CASE OF EXAGGERATION

Most of the lies we tell are harmless white ones, of course. We all can – and do – exaggerate. But perhaps the most common white lie we tell is when we shave the odd unwanted year off our ages. 1984's winner of the Booker-McConnell Prize, Professor Anita Brookner, found her 'official' age the subject of much ribald comment. She wrote to *The Times* in November 1984:

> Allow me to put the record straight. I am 46, and have been for some years past.

Actually, this was a white lie too. Professor Brookner had admitted to 52 in the 1980 edition of *Who's Who*, where she gave her year of birth as 1928. When the 1981 edition came out, eager readers found that she had none-too-subtly lopped 10 years off her age, claiming 1938 as her year of birth. One waits with trepidation for the moment when she will have been born in 1948.

Following her lead was a former Mrs Ronald Reagan, actress Jane Wyman, who in March 1985 invited friends to her 31st birthday party. The *Falcon Crest* star was, in fact, 71, but declared:

> I don't count the years before I was converted to Catholicism.

Others, of course, go the other way:

> I'm 94 going on 95.
>
> *Peggy Lee on the eve of her 65th birthday, May 1984*

But as I've said 1000 times before in this chapter, don't we all exaggerate?

Miss World, Sarah-Jane Hutt, told us in August 1984 how she was

The loneliest girl in the universe.

Of course!

Men are scared of me . . .
she purred, adding:
They don't approach me because they think I am on a pedestal and I am too much of a challenge. But I am an ordinary person and I would love to talk to men on an ordinary level.

Everybody say awh . . .

I am middle-aged, and I like middle age. And one day I'm going to be seriously old, and that will be terrific too, because I'll be wise – not old-old, but alive-old.
Linda Evans, 'Krystle' of 'Dynasty', December 1984

Prize for the most over-the-top statement of the year must surely go to Bob Geldof for his unwise words at the British Rock and Pop Awards ceremony in February 1985:

> Compared to Ethiopia, what happened in Europe 40 years ago was a perverted tea party.

The BBC sagely edited out his words for a repeat showing on BBC2.

When he became (briefly) engaged to Elizabeth Taylor in December 1984, New York playboy Dennis Stein also went a bit over the top with:

> Elizabeth has a magic wand of happiness that she has struck me with.

If in doubt, exaggerate:

> I didn't have my first bath until I was 42.
>
> *Frank (Lord) Chapple, 1984*

Senator Edward Kennedy was upset in January 1985, during a tour of South Africa, about a number of jibes aimed at his ballooning figure. He promised to shed at least 35 lb. One newspaper report particularly upset him. It said:

> Watching Kennedy get out of a chair is like watching Russia get out of Afghanistan.

However, perhaps the best white lie of the year came in October 1984 from Mrs Helen Kime, wife of a Wiltshire antiques dealer. Receiving from her husband for a birthday present a 350-year-old dead elm weighing three tons, she proffered hearty thanks, saying:

> It is better than something like a Hoover.

Sometimes it's hard to put your finger on the exact exaggeration contained in a statement: all you know is that it's in there somewhere . . .

> What I would really like is a honeymoon on a houseboat on a lake in Kashmir.
>
> *Slightly distant dream of murderer Ronnie Kray, now in Broadmoor, on his forthcoming marriage to divorcee Elaine Mildener, January 1985*

> I'll bet we were the best treated hostages anywhere in the world.
>
> *Ian Fenton, 57, an engineer from Bournemouth, after being freed in May 1984 in Angola at the end of 11 weeks of captivity in the hands of Unita guerillas*

> I know it's a strange thing to say. But the hijackers were very nice people.
>
> *Miss Jane Wallington, gushing in August 1984 about the three Moslem terrorists who hijacked the Air France 737 on which she was travelling*

She added:

> They were very friendly. They were so relaxed, running up and down, telling jokes. They would make tremendous stewards.

Miss Wallington admitted she was a bit concerned, however, that the 'stewards' were lighting cigarettes with a lighter in one hand while holding a petrol bomb in the other. Definitely *not* in the 'I'm Mandy – Fly Me' handbook.

Some more exaggeration – in both directions:

I've had a disturbed night.

Cabinet minister John Biffen after his rooms had been nearly blown apart by the Brighton hotel bomb, October 1984

This is the handshake of the century.

Rauf Denktash, as the leader of 120,000 Turkish Cypriots clasped the hands of Greek Cypriot President Spyros Kyprianou, January 1985

My boys love it. If they were to be asked what they would most reluctantly give up it would be the cold bath every morning.

Mr John Knock, headmaster of Housham Hall School, near York, July 1984, after school inspectors had said the daily ritual for boys aged 5–13 should be 'revised'

THE PAPER THAT PLAYS IT STRAIGHT.

Strapline in the 'Sun', September 1984

Sportsmen are, shall we say, 'not immune' to exaggeration.

If Wales went to war with Russia tomorrow, I honestly reckon Wales would have a bloody good chance.

Andrew Slack, Wallabies captain, before game against Wales

She's a natural. If she'd taken up the game a little earlier, she might have been a champ.

Snooker ace John Virgo, June 1984, with a little Royal overstatement, after inviting the Queen Mother to join a game at the Jersey Park Centre

The official ranking puts Steve Davis at No. 1 – quite right. He's won the tournaments and the points to earn it. But in my own ranking, based on natural ability, inborn talent – call it what you like – I can't rate him higher than fifth.

Snooker player Willie Thorne, November 1984; naturally, he put himself at No. 1 – 'jointly with Alex Higgins and Jimmy White'.

On Steve Davis, just to underline the point, Thorne added:

He only just makes it at No. 5.

Hall of Infamy

I once told a joke and it was very dirty and I was sick for a month afterwards. Honest.

Bette Midler

I may have to give it all up. It's the love scenes, you see. I find that nowadays I can only manage one take.

Roger Moore, after making 'Octopussy'

People who don't have it think beauty is a blessing. Actually, it's a kind of sentence – a confinement.

Candice Bergen, August 1980

He may be my oldest boyfriend but he definitely acts as if he's the youngest. On a scale of one to 10, George is 10.

Kim High (22), on her new love George Burns (83), October 1979

I would give myself 5.9 out of six.

Labour leader Neil Kinnock, à la *Torvill and Dean, returning from what everyone else considered a lacklustre tour of the US, February 1984. In the Commons Tory backbenchers entered into the spirit, holding up cards giving him 0.1 and even 0.0.*

We are the greatest wee nation ever Goad put braith in.

Ally MacLeod

I am my own jailer. I'd be quite happy to live in a three-bedroomed council house.

Marchioness of Tavistock, 1978

Shergar: Biggest Disappearance Since the Resurrection.
'Sunday Times' headline, March 1983

One specialist shoved an Eiffel Tower up my arse with a light at the end of it – rather painful.
Noel Coward

If you guys think you are fighting over here, you should see them battling for Cabbage Patch dolls back home.
Bob Hope entertaining US marines in Beirut, December 1983

The balls of Bob Menzies
Are wrinkled and crinkled
Curvaceous, capacious
As the dome of St Paul's.
The crowds they all muster
To gape at that cluster
And gaze at the size of
Those bloody great balls!
Australian (where else?) anthem for their favourite Prime Minister

I shall lie doggo for a while.
Lord Lucan, last letter to friends, June 1975

SLIGHT EXAGGERATION

14 THE TWENTY GREATEST FORKED TONGUES – A PERSONAL SELECTION

1 At various times in the next 20 or 30 years I think it is reasonable to anticipate that I will be among the leadership of the Labour Party, but, as for being leader, I can't see that happening.

Neil Kinnock, 1980

2 No woman in my time will be Prime Minister or Foreign Secretary – not the top jobs. Anyway, I wouldn't want to be Prime Minister. You have to give yourself one hundred per cent.

Margaret Thatcher, 1969

3 It is vital, in my opinion, that tennis maintains a strong and watchful stand against swearing.

John McEnroe, 1983

4 I wouldn't act again. Not for anything. I don't want to be looked upon as a pretty, brainless idiot any more.

Victoria Principal, who later became Pam Ewing in 'Dallas', talking in 1976

5 I am an actor and I'm going to stick to acting.

Ronald Reagan to Sheilah Graham, back in the 1950s

6 I'll never play Bond again.

Sean Connery after 'You Only Live Twice' and again after 'Diamonds are Forever'. Small wonder they called his next Bond film 'Never Say Never Again'

7 This is my last concert. I have retired.

Frank Sinatra, Los Angeles, June 1971. (If he didn't keep retiring, who'd want to go to his comebacks?)

8 The question of Cecil Parkinson's resignation does not – and will not – arise.

Downing Street spokesman, October 1983

9 I know your frequent use of the word 'invasion'. This was a rescue mission.

President Reagan to journalists after US 'intervention' in Grenada, November 1983

10 Laker Airways are perfectly healthy. Rumours of the airline going bankrupt are malicious and fictitious. There is absolutely no question of the airline folding. The only liquidation around Gatwick is the rain.

Laker Airways spokesman, January 1982, 16 days before the airline crashed owing $350 million

11 CHARLES TO MARRY ASTRID – OFFICIAL
Prince Charles is to marry Princes Marie-Astrid of Luxembourg. The formal announcement will be made from Buckingham Palace next Monday.

'Daily Express' splash story, June 1977

12 There is no romance and there are no grounds for these rumours of a romance between Lieutenant Mark Phillips and myself. I cannot understand why there is all this interest in our going riding together.

Princess Anne, March 1973

13 BOB WOODWARD: Have you ever organised wiretaps yourself?

HENRY KISSINGER: Almost never.

Quoted in W. Shawcross, 'Sideshow: Kissinger, Nixon and the Destruction of Cambodia', 1979

14 Princess Diana will give birth to a beautiful daughter, with blue eyes and a lovely mixture of high spirits and determination. Charles will be delighted with the new addition. They will very probably call her Alice Louise, but she will have a family nickname like Bubbles.

Roger Elliot, 'News of the World' astrologer, November 1983, one of several Fleet Street pundits who confidently awaited a new princess. In fact, he *was a son, and wasn't called Alice, Louise or Bubbles, but Henry (family nickname: Harry)*

15 Q. Mr Foot, do you believe you'll win tomorrow?
A. Yes, we do indeed.

Michael Foot, ITN News, June 8, 1983 (he later said he knew all along he'd lose)

16 There can be no whitewash in the White House.

Richard Nixon, nationwide TV broadcast, April 30, 1973

17 I haven't changed in 40 years. I'm still a disaster.

Harold Robbins, December 1983

18 Yuri Andropov is going to be around for a while.

Conclusion of a special investigation by a high-powered team of doctors from US Intelligence reported in 'Newsweek' magazine, July 1983. He died in February 1984, after serving the shortest term up until that time of any Soviet leader

19 Rod and I really are the Liz Taylor and Richard Burton of the '70s – but without the yuckiness. I mean, I think we

have more class, more style. People say we are pop's most charismatic couple and it's true.

Britt Ekland, 1981, on her romance with Rod Stewart

20 Lech Walesa is not under arrest. He is staying at a government guest house.

Polish martial law spokesman

15 TONGUE-TIGHT

One type of Forked Tongue comes quite by accident. The verbal slip-up. The linguistic gaffe. Commentators and football managers are famed for them. Politicians dread them. The rest of us love them. The results are usually hilarious.

In December 1984 Ronald Reagan rose to welcome as White House guest of honour the President of Venezuela. He rescued from his jacket pocket a speech that began:

Your Highness. . . .

Then he realised: this wasn't his speech for the Venezuelan leader. He had put on, by mistake, the suit which he had worn the week before when his guest had been the Grand Duke of Luxembourg. 'In his usual skilled way,' said a doting aide, 'he just ad-libbed his way out of trouble.'

That was necessary, too, for his running mate, Vice-President George Bush, who told a gathering of redneck supporters after his TV debate with Geraldine Ferraro in October 1984:

We tried to kick a little ass last night!

He then realised what he'd said and asked if the radio and TV microphones had picked up his remark. They had.

Veteran broadcaster David Jacobs made an uncertain start as chairman of a new TVS show, *Questions*, in March 1985, introducing Dr David Owen as

Dr David Steel.

In the same month, new US Attorney General Edwin Meese III told reporters:

I intend to revitalise the 10th Commandment.

(He meant the 10th *Amendment.*) And ITN newscaster

Carol Barnes informed viewers in January 1985 that

It'll be a cloudy day with sunny smells

while an Independent Radio News announcer told in November how

There has been trouble at C.W.M. in South Wales.

It wasn't an engineering firm. It was the pit village of Cwm near Pontypridd. Thames ITV newscaster Tina Jenkins told us in January 1985 that

A rubbery suspect is still holding police at bay in Streatham.

Slippery customer that.

Weatherman Tony Target let forth the ultimate in December 1984, on the Points West programme, after calling a colleague by the wrong name:

Oh, bugger!

A sign outside the North Shore Methodist Church, Blackpool, prior to the October 1984 Labour Party conference, read:

Preacher: The Rev. Peter Shilling BD
The Rt Hon Neil Kinnock MP
Mrs Gladys Kinnock

Nice one, Glad.

Method. Prepare dumplings by making up two escaped prisoners described by police as desperate and dangerous . . . Bring to the boil and stir in the arrests . . . Sprinkle with parsley and serve hot.

Screen muddle from 'Oracle', ITV teletext service, February 1985

The Olympic Games brought a fair crop of sporting clangers:

The reason she won is that the others, quite simply, couldn't catch her.

Hamilton Bland, BBC swimming commentator

For my money, his left leg is definitely not right . . .

Harry Carpenter

Back home, linkman Terry Wogan was not to be left out:

. . . this is the one in which Carl Lewis goes for the hat-trick of four gold medals.

It's the highest score so far . . . and that puts her in the lead.

Alan Weeks, BBC

It was a throw that no one could catch.

Summariser David Hemery on Tessa Sanderson's winning javelin attempt

She's fully exposed herself at the front.

Brendan Foster of marathon-winner Joan Benoit

But back to Britain and football for the best in tongue-tight sporting gaffemanship.

I am a firm believer that if you score one goal, the other team has to score two to win.

Sheffield Wednesday manager Howard Wilkinson

He has completed a mission-impossible this week.

Spurs manager Peter Shreeves on Glenn Hoddle's return from injury, February 1985

At the start of the 1984/85 season, second-division Brighton ran a special feature in their match programme on favourite soccer clangers. Among them:

Most of the people who can remember when we were a great club are dead.

Jack Dunnett, chairman of Notts County

Obviously for Scunthorpe it would be a nice scalp to put Wimbledon on their bottoms.

Dave Bassett, manager of Wimbledon

. . . and with eight minutes left, the game could be won or lost in the next five or ten minutes.

Jimmy Armfield, BBC Radio 2

We could be putting the hammer in Luton's coffin.

Ray Wilkins, Manchester United, speaking on 'Match of the Day'

The *Daily Star* followed this up in October 1984 by asking readers to submit their best sporting tongue-ties. Among their bumper harvest:

Williams beat Shilton from 35 yards. And you don't beat Shilton from 35 yards.

Peter Jones, Radio 2

There'll be more football in a moment. But first we've got highlights of the Scottish League Cup.

Gary Newbon, ITV

That's a strange sight. Lester Pigott walking down the course without a horse between his legs.

John Oaksey, ITV

Mickey Thomas has scored on his debut for Chelsea. That's his first goal for the club.

David Coleman, BBC

The Test Match begins in ten minutes. That's our time, of course.

David Coleman, BBC

The toilet rolls have been removed and the game is now back in motion.

David Coleman, BBC

Hall of Infamy

And now coming up to the rider jump there's a waterless horse out in front.

Raymond Glendenning, BBC commentator, on the Grand National

It's not for myself that I'm worried. But if you go into that dressing room there, it's like a mortgage.

Joe Smith, Blackpool manager, after 5–1 defeat

Remember, postcards only, please. The winner will be the first one opened.

Brian Moore, ITV

Some of our fans are very partesian.

Manny Cussins, Leeds United chairman, asked about crowd trouble

For those of you watching in black and white – Spurs are in the all-yellow strip.

John Motson, BBC

. . . your carpenter, Harry Commentator . . .

Linkman Frank Bough, BBC

He's brought a new harmonium to the dressing room.

Joe Smith, Blackpool manager, on a new signing

And Allan Lamb is out caught – just as he was nearing the middle of a great innings.

Jim Laker

Don't let's talk about a bumpy pitch at this level.
Lawrie McMenemy

Play has ended here at Southampton, but they play till seven o'clock up at Edgbaston, so over there now for some more balls from Rex Alston.
Brian Johnston, BBC

SPORTING SLIP-UPS

16 EXCUSES

'A lie is an abomination to the Lord,' said Adlai Stevenson, 'and a very present help in trouble.' There was certainly plenty of 'present help' during the year – and some excuses were, well, masterstrokes of invention. One-legged drunken driver Gary Livingstone, who had twice the legal limit of alcohol in his blood, had a novel defence. Said Mr Peter Clark, defending, in July 1984:

> The reading was higher than it would be for a man with two legs. Gary has less blood in his body.

Bristol magistrates were unimpressed, fining Mr Livingstone £210 and banning him from driving for 15 months, after he had admitted driving when over the alcohol limit, careless driving and failing to stop after an accident.

Duran Duran star Simon Le Bon gave this reason in December 1984 for not marrying his long-standing girlfriend Claire Stansfield:

> Marriage is a very serious matter, and I'm not in a very serious mood these days.

> I only collapsed from fatigue and all the excitement.
>
> *Ex-soccer star George Best, November 1984, explaining his non-appearance in court on a drink-driving charge*

> I think I have an allergy to certain types of drugs.
>
> *Liza Minnelli, November 1984, after four weeks at the Betty Ford Clinic in California*

Accused of calling an umpire 'a f***ing faggot' during the December 1984 Davis Cup match between the USA and

Sweden, tennis ace Jimmy Connors explained:

> I have always moaned and groaned to myself throughout my career.

Asked on TV why he had a *penchant* for patting ladies' rear ends – cameras had twice caught him touching fellow-Liberals in a familiar way – John Turner, newly installed Premier of Canada, said in July 1984:

> I am a man of warmth. These were gestures of friendship, gestures of camaraderie. There was no disrespect.

Alastair Reid, a writer for the *New Yorker* who was exposed in June 1984 as having fabricated articles about Spain, told the *Wall Street Journal*:

> Whether the bar existed or not was irrelevant to what I was after. If one wants to write about Spain, the facts won't get you anywhere.

In early 1985 the Meteorological Office indulged in some pure slush when twice they were caught out over sudden massive snowfalls which they had failed to forecast. A spokesman explained in January 1985 why they had not foreseen Arctic blizzards which had paralysed the West Country:

> We were right about there being a lot of snow, but it wasn't in the right area.

In February 1985 BBC weatherman Bill Giles said, after another round of blizzards, which had brought snow 10 inches deep to the Midlands:

> In fact there wasn't all that much. What there was drifted badly in the high winds.

Venessa Llewellyn, wife of former 'seducer of the Valleys' Dai Llewellyn, bared all about her life with 'Dirty Dai' in a Sunday newspaper in December 1984. She agreed it would be right to say that, when she moved into his flat in Harley Street, everything was not idyllic:

> One morning as I was leaving for work I saw a girl arriving at the door. When I returned in the afternoon she was still there. *Dai said that she had just come to collect something but I knew better.*

Clever girl that. She'll go far. But you know these complicated living arrangements . . . In March 1985 Linn Ullmann, 18, told how when she was young her actress mother Liv had explained away having a boyfriend stay the night in her bedroom. Mother told daughter:

> He's got to sleep in my bedroom because he's afraid of the dark.

Officialdom too comes up with the most incredible excuses to explain foolish behaviour. It was revealed in March 1985 that Labour-controlled Islington council had put up a disturbed 17-year-old girl for five months in no less than 18 different hotels. She had been given £7 pocket money a day and unlimited use of the telephone. When a council finance officer queried the exorbitant cost of endless telephone calls, a senior social worker turned in a memorandum saying:

> The telephone is one way of keeping her occupied and under control when her behaviour reaches manic proportions.

Next time you need a free telephone call, try putting it to Islington that you're feeling a bit manic.

Lou Macari, new manager of Swindon Town, was fined £80 and given a week's driving ban after having been trapped by police while driving at 101mph on the M5. The former Manchester United and Scotland star told them:

I was in a hurry to complete my first signing.

His old boss Tommy Docherty had a typically wry comment:

Fancy that! He never went that fast when he played for me.

Mrs Jean Clayden, 42, a horsewoman friend of Prince Philip, was a witness in a theft case at Chelmsford Crown Court in January 1985. The accused was odd-job man David Pearce, whom she accused of stealing her pet Yorkshire terrier, Barney, and demanding £2000 in return. Said Mrs Clayden:

We weren't exactly lovers although we were having sex.

Peter Hunt, 35, redundant machine operator, fined £30 by Chorley, Lancashire, magistrates in March 1984 for speeding told the court that his baby daughter Victoria had become hungry and that his wife had started to breast-feed her. He said he drove at 50mph:

To spare my wife's embarrassment.

In June 1984 Mr Clifford Henry, 23, was granted a conditional discharge by Clerkenwell magistrates for possessing cannabis. He said:

It's my hay fever. The only relief I can get is from a cannabis cigarette. I am teetotal and a nonsmoker really.

Mr Mark Romer, the magistrate, told him:

Try the chemist next time.

Henry Burnaby Harrod, 19-year-old grandson of Lord Lambton, was fined £800 by Horseferry magistrates in August 1984 for possessing cocaine from Peru. He said:

I thought I was helping someone out there, because it's their livelihood, and poverty is something else out there.

Mr Ladislaw Mark of Sofia, Bulgaria, jailed in Spring 1984 for trying to steal the body of a young girl from a mortuary, told the court:

I wanted it as a figurehead for my fishing boat.

And finally there was the Lincolnshire man who, in Spring 1984, pleading guilty to possessing an offensive weapon (a knuckleduster), told the court:

I have been studying knuckleduster technique in order to help my family survive after a nuclear war.

Hall of Infamy

Excuse me not inviting you in. I'm in bed with somebody I don't know very well.

Beryl Reid, getting rid of unwelcome visitors

I wasn't kissing her. I was whispering in her mouth.

Chico Marx, when caught by his wife cuddling up to a chorus girl

A divorce judge heard how an actress had arrived home late one night, and that her husband had barred entry to the bedroom. There was a girl with him. He told his wife:

She was only helping hang some curtains.

Said Mr Justice Faulks:

That may have been right. But it seems an odd time of day for that sort of thing.

In 1983 Glenn Massey, 24, of Coalville, Leicestershire, admitted travelling illegally on the roof of the Birmingham to Swansea Inter-City express as it passed under at least three tunnels. He told officials:

I was looking for the bar.

A South African fined for pointing a loaded pistol at his estranged wife told the court in Johannesburg:

I was trying for a reconciliation.

MASTERS OF INVENTION?

Hall of Infamy

When police in Ventura, California, apprehended a woman driver involved in a two-car collision, they found her totally in the nude. Booked for reckless driving, she told officers, according to the *San Francisco Chronicle*:

> When I began my drive, I *thought* I was a camel in Morocco. But when I saw palm trees lining the streets, I was convinced.

At Houston, Texas, 82-year-old grandmother Laura Clark, accused of growing six 'pot' plants in her back garden, said:

> I thought I was growing herbs for my arthritis.

Found trapped in a chimney at the Bernard Engraving Company in Los Angeles and asked what he was doing there, Peter Sargent, a 29-year-old hobo, told police:

> We were playing charades and I was supposed to be Santa Claus.

He was held on suspicion of burglary.

Alfred Madsen, 21, who confessed in a New York court to stealing 3,000,000 dollars' worth of gems from a Manhattan jewellers, said:

> I got impatient waiting for my girlfriend to finish in the bath.

A confessed rapist claimed mitigating circumstances:

> It was half a bottle of cough mixture I had earlier. I was only trying to cure a sore throat.

A 19-year-old housewife from Memphis told a grand jury that she had had sex with 5000 policemen in three years. Her excuse:

> After an hour and a half trapped in a sauna bath I changed from a devout Catholic housewife into a nymphomaniac.

'Sex in chains' Mormon missionary Kirk Anderson, asked in court in 1977 why he had succumbed to the advances of Miss Joyce McKinney (assisted by a male friend), said:

> After they tied down one leg and then the other, I could not resist the rest.

After a raid on a Los Angeles 'auction', police bought a man for $16 and then brought a prosecution against what they called 'sado-masochistic homosexuals' under an old slavery statute. Gay leaders protested:

> This was not a slave market. It was a fund-raising event for a VD clinic.

More celebrated was the case of suburban madam Mrs Cynthia Payne, made famous by the house slogan: 'We also accept luncheon vouchers.' After the police had raided Mrs Payne's establishment and rounded up the customers, one 70-year-old gentleman excused himself with the memorable line:

> I'm a bit past it. I'm only here because it's a Christmas party.

MORE MASTERS OF INVENTION?

17 LYING IN THE SUN: FORTY WHOPPERS FROM THE HOLIDAY BROCHURES

In March 1985 a report from the British Advertising Standards Authority blew the gaff on the embellishment, deliberate deception and often downright lying by the holiday industry. The all-time classic example was provided by the Manor Court Hotel at Moretonhampstead, Devon, whose literature boasted of the 'secluded beaches nearby'. That's stretching a point, rapped the ASA: the beach is *17 miles* away!

Picking a way through those cunningly phrased and always inviting paragraphs from the tour operators is always a minefield for those not fully on their guard. Here is a definitive guide for fun- and sun-seekers abroad.

What they say	**What they mean**
small fishing village	no beach
sophisticated resort	sprawl of concrete-tower hotels
new resort	dirt roads, scaffolding everywhere
popular resort	unbearably crowded
ever-popular resort	even more crowded
serene	ordinary
traditional surroundings	poor sewerage
spacious hotel	reception area like aircraft hangar
recently constructed	unfinished
recently modernised	half-built
modern architecture	utility, no carpets

What they say	What they mean
composite hotel	five-minute walk to dining-rooms, etc. – which are in another building
long-established hotel	run-down
pleasant setting/quietly situated	miles from anywhere
centrally situated	on the busiest traffic intersection in town
old part of town	between wasteland and abattoir, five miles from the beach
overlooking the sea	inland and halfway up a mountain, five miles from the beach
sea view	distant view of briny between two tower apartment blocks – if you stand on a chair and peer hard
offers every comfort	small lounge with two armchairs, bars open until late
very friendly	rowdy
fun for all the family	lots of slot machines
dreamlike atmosphere	nothing to do except drink and lie in the sun

What they say	What they mean
you'll soon get to know your fellow holidaymakers	walls are wafer-thin
blissful sense of peace	dead boring
daring	rude games
lively	nonstop drinking and drunks
meet like-minded people	lots of casual sex
action-packed	even more casual sex
freestyle	'gays' welcome
fun-filled	no sleep until dawn – whether you like it or not
excellent choice for families	screaming kids everywhere
excellent as an excursion centre	the place itself is so dreadful that everyone rushes to go somewhere else
pleasant promenade	dual-carriageway main coast road
colourful shops	rip-off gift stores
old-fashioned shopping centre	expensive
sophisticated shopping centre	extremely expensive
irresistible to bargain hunters	crawling with pestering touts

What they say	What they mean
bars and restaurants catering for all tastes	English pubs, hamburger and chip stands, catering for the hoi polloi
looks too good to be true	the touched-up photos in the brochure *are* too good to be true!

18 U-TURNS

Only a couple of years ago, President Reagan was saying some pretty uncomplimentary things about Russia – you know, like, 'The Soviet Union is an evil empire that reserves the right to lie, to cheat . . .' and 'this totalitarian darkness . . . they are the focus of evil in the modern world.' All this had changed in the run-up to the Geneva arms talks, however. Said Mr Reagan in October 1984:

It is clear there is not a great distance between us.

Of course not, of course not!

A few glasses of wine and I'm anybody's for the night.

Wham! star George Michael, January 1984

Perhaps the year's most amazing somersault came from the BBC, who in early 1984 banned the No. 1 hit record 'Relax' by Frankie Goes to Hollywood on the grounds that

> The lyrics are sexually explicit and not suitable for a programme transmitted in family viewing time.

A film showing Frankie perform the 'offensive number' was shown for the first time on Christmas Day within five minutes of the Queen's broadcast, which included scenes from the day of the christening of Prince Harry. And if that isn't family viewing time, what is?

We're a bit fussy who we sleep with.

Wham! star George Michael, March 1985

> The US Government has scrupulously avoided taking sides in the Salvadorian election.
>
> *State Department spokesman John Hughes, May 4, 1984*

> In so far as the State Department is concerned, there's absolutely no funding to Mr Duarte or indeed, any party. Obviously we can't speak for the CIA.
>
> *State Department spokesman John Hughes, May 12, 1984*

George Best is a pathetic playboy who ruined a brilliant

football career through booze. . . . But I wonder why the law felt it necessary to treat this faded superstar like a desperate criminal on the run. George Best is a sad, sorry figure who needs help. There's no need to treat him like Public Enemy Number One.

'Plain' John Smith, lead item to 'Straight Talk', 'Sunday People', December 1984

It's a bit early to be handing out annual awards. But George Best has already walked away with my nomination for Yawn of the Year. Mr Best is currently holidaying on a sunkissed island. For all our sakes, I suggest he stops there . . . I'll willingly contribute . . . Coughing up a few extra bob to keep an ocean or two between us and Boring Old Bestie would be an absolute bargain.

'Plain' John Smith, lead item to 'Straight Talk', 'Sunday People', January 1985

Come on, like you said, there's no need to treat him as Public Enemy Number One!

Zola Budd has renounced her South African citizenship to make it clear that she is in Britain and in Britain to stay.

'Daily Mail', May 1984

Zola Budd is to quit international athletics in her adopted Britain and remain in her native South Africa.

'Daily Mail', November 1984

My final wish is to be treated and accepted as any other British athlete.

Zola Budd, after returning to Britain to run, January 1985

Considering the state of him he worked wonders. I'd give him nine out of ten for effort and seven for style.

Lynn Brown, Bristol student, on a night of passion with Wham! star Andrew Ridgeley, 'News of the World', March 1985

He was so drunk he couldn't even raise a smile.

Lynn Brown, Bristol student, on a night of passion with Wham! star Andrew Ridgeley, quoted by her landlord Jan Smeeton in the 'Sunday People', March 1985

All very confusing.

Political U-turn of the year was undoubtedly Education Minister Sir Keith Joseph's mighty climbdown on his plans to make parents pay more towards student grants. In December 1984 he told the *Sunday Telegraph* ('Joseph ready to resign over students' cash') that he would quit rather than bow to backbench pressure to scrap his scheme to raise money for scientific research through a grants squeeze. The following day a briefing to journalists said that

> The government is standing firm and will not yield much, if at all.

Two days later Sir Keith faced a meeting of Conservative backbenchers at which, it was alleged, 'there was blood on the walls'. And the day after that, on December 6, he stood up in the Commons and said:

> I recognise the concern expressed in this House and elsewhere, that the increase was too sharp and the notice too short.

On-off engagement of the year was that between Joan Collins, shimmering 51-year-old star of *Dynasty*, and Peter Holm, 37, described as her 'business manager'. According to Nigel Dempster in the *Daily Mail*, just 48 hours after announcing their betrothal Miss Collins had thrown her £100,000 ring back at Mr Holm and told him:

> The whole thing is off.

The couple had apparently flown in to the Caribbean island of Antigua to be the major guests at the opening of Mr Peter de Savary's St James's Club, but Mr Holm had refused to pose for photographers unless a fee were paid. It was this which was said to have infuriated the never publicity-shy Miss Collins. Reported a fellow guest:

> Only when Holm relented a day later and agreed to have the pictures taken for nothing did Joan decide to become re-engaged.

Imagine a Mr Joan Collins opting for 'no publicity'!

> I am on strike. I'll never play for Southampton again. I have kicked my last ball for them.
>
> *Fiery redhead soccer player Mark Wright, November 1984, after revelations of a dressing-room punch-up with manager Lawrie McMenemy. He was back in December after donating an £8,000 fee from a Sunday newspaper to the Ethiopian famine appeal*

> I've made up my mind to stay single for the next five years. I'm having a good time for the first time in my life . . . I'm footloose and fancy free . . . it's difficult to build a relationship up when you are flying about all over the place. And that's going to be the scene for me for the foreseeable future.
>
> *Marti Caine, February 1984. Six months later she married director Ken Ives*

19 DOUBLESPEAK

Richard Halverson, Chaplain to the US Senate, issued this prayer for the 'word merchants' in the chamber in April 1984:

> Help them to appreciate the power of words . . . to honour, to disparage; to encourage, to disappoint; to comfort, to embarrass; to edify, to offend; to strengthen, to weaken; to motivate, to immobilise; to give hope, to frustrate; to purify, to pollute; to build, to destroy.

Doublespeak, the 1980s way to lie – using the power of language to bluff, to distort, to cover up the truth – didn't desert us in 1984 or the first half of 1985.

Here's Jones's report on the top fog phrases of the year – and, if you haven't worked them out yet, their *true* meaning.

We are *on course*/we are *on target*
Line used by Thatcher/Lawson/Treasury, among many others. Means: We are in terrible trouble but, like Mr Micawber, hope something will still turn up.

The firm is undergoing *shrinkage*
Means: Closure in whole or part.

That is a very *simplistic* view
Used (unwisely) by Roy Hattersley to Lord Denning (to name just one case). Means: OK, it's true, but we're not going to admit it.

He was *forthcoming and flexible*
Used by Tory MP Sir Kenneth Lewis to describe the U-turn by Sir Keith Joseph on student grants. Means: Did a complete somersault.

We shall continue to pursue *progressive policies*
Means: We shall continue to pursue reactionary policies, true to our party dogma.

The talks were *businesslike*
Used in a communique to describe Margaret Thatcher's meeting with Soviet politburo member Mikhail Gorbachev. Means: heated but determined exchange. To be distinguished from: 'frank' (full-scale shouting match), 'constructive' (polite exchange of differing views), 'comradely' (Soviet way of saying that, for example, Poland or Czechoslovakia has agreed to do as told), and 'complete identity of views' (total subservience to Soviet line).

The *heterosexual community*
BBC minority-unitspeak for the 90 per cent of us who, through no fault of our own, are *not* homosexuals (sorry, members of the 'gay community').

Full inquiry
Have you ever heard of a 'half inquiry'?

Let me say this . . .
Used by, it seems, all members of the NUM side during the coal dispute. Means: I'm about to tell a whopper.

No disrespect . . .
Used by TV interviewers and their victims. 'No disrespect, Mr Scargill, but . . .'; 'No disrespect, Mr McGregor, but . . .' Means: I'm about to insult you.

Could not *beneficially be developed*
The Coal Board's crucial phrase separating the two sides in the pit strike. Means: We reserve the right to close pits when we want.

This battle has reached a *crucial stage*
Used by Tony Benn, MP, January 1985. Means: We've lost. In March 1985, just before the majority of his members deserted him, Arthur Scargill had a variant: 'The battle has entered *a new era*.'

We will enter into talks *without preconditions*
Used by Arthur Scargill and the NUM executive after the return-to-work movement gained momentum, January 1985. Means: We're now looking for a face-saving formula.

We want *meaningful peace talks*
Used by the Coal Board, January 1985. Means: We want complete surrender. Mrs Thatcher's version of demanding capitulation was: 'Fudged settlements never work.'

And the above list does not even mention Scargill's famous and ludicrous catch-phrase: 'Let me be frank . . . I want to make one thing perfectly clear.' The only thing he ever made perfectly clear was that he would on no account answer the questions put to him.

During the year, I was on the receiving end of an

astonishing 'no comment' from one leading politician. I won't say who it is, but you may be able to guess. The exchange, on a purely internal political matter, nothing sensational at all, went something like this:

Q. Are you able to talk about this?
A. No, I do not want to talk about it.
Q. Well, are you prepared to talk about it off the record?
A. It is not a subject I talk about, either on or off the record.
Q. Well, can I quote you on the record as saying that you are not prepared to talk about it?
A. When I said I was not prepared to talk about it either on the record or off the record, that was off the record.

And so to the wider world of doublespeak. In March 1985 the British Ministry of Defence admitted that nuclear tests had been considered 30 years before off Wick in the extreme northeast of Scotland, but allayed any fears we might have had:

They were not designed to create a mushroom-cloud situation

Said the men from the Ministry:

They would have created a neutron environment.

So now you know.

In October 1984 an 89-page CIA manual instructing Nicaraguan rebels on terrorist tactics surfaced in Washington. The White House was embarrassed, particularly when the manual talked of how to 'Neutralise' local officials – meaning, presumably, assassinate them. President Reagan said there was nothing in the manual about assassinations. He added:

I think you're going to find that it was all a great big scare.

A misunderstanding had arisen, he claimed, because the word 'remove' had been mistranslated as 'neutralise' in the Spanish version. Asked as he campaigned at John Wayne's birthplace in Winterset, Iowa, how you 'removed' someone from office without violence, the President cheerily replied:

You just say to the fellow that's sitting there in the office: 'You're not in office any more.'

Mr Reagan flannels. His deputy, George Bush, has another tactic: he speaks in riddles. In August 1984, at the Los Angeles Olympics, the Vice-President told how the faces of America's athletes were filled with

Optimism and determinism

as well as exhorting reporters to

Elevate it, elevate it, elevate it

whatever that should mean. Perhaps the most inelevatable Bush statement of the 1984 campaign came when Walter Mondale demanded an apology for Bush's accusation that Mondale had said American marines 'died in shame' in the Lebanon. Said the Vice-President:

I'll lay my record on any forum, whatever it is, on my manhood, up against his.

The mind runs riot.

What's needed is some plain speaking, of course. One of the worst examples of official gobbledegook unearthed by the Plain English Campaign during the year was an official letter to residents from the London Borough of Ealing which began:

Take notice that for the purpose of enabling the Council of the London Borough of Ealing to make Article 4

> Direction relating to property at the above address and to serve copies of Article 4 Direction in accordance with Article 4 of the Town and Country Planning General Development Order 1977, the Council pursuant to section 284 of the said Act . . .

A Co-op dairy in the South of England issued customers in December 1984 with a leaflet detailing its Christmas milk deliveries:

> Deliveries on Saturday will be as normal which includes Sunday's milk. Deliveries commencing Sunday 23rd will be one day in advance. On Sunday milk will be delivered which is Monday's milk. Milk delivered on Monday (Christmas Eve) will be Tuesday's (Christmas Day) milk. No delivery on Tuesday (Christmas Day). Deliveries on Wednesday (Boxing Day) will be normal and from that day onwards will be as usual.

Still puzzled?

> The Jumbo puzzle, which appeared on page D1 of Thursday's edition, actually was the puzzle scheduled to appear today. The Jumbo originally scheduled to appear Thursday as well as the answers to Wednesday's puzzle are on page E1 today. The answers to the puzzle published today appeared Thursday, and the answers to the puzzle published Thursday will appear Saturday.
>
> *Arizona Republic*

Finally, the Official Forked Tongues expanded guide to the worst examples of doublespeak in public life today . . . and the real meaning of those buzzwords.

What they say	What they mean
neutralisation	annihilation
emergent nation	backward country
aerial reconnaissance/ reconnaissance in force/ air support	bombing
incontinent ordnance	bombing of schools, hospitals, etc., by mistake
warrantless investigation/ uncontested physical search/surreptitious entry	break-in
highly confidential source	bug
plumber	burglar
intelligence-gathering/ black-bag job/convert operation/technical trespass	burglary
bilateral orchidectomy	castration
personal assistant (special activities)	cook
negative patient outcome	death
strongman	dictator
catering controller	dinner lady
eyeball-to-eyeball situation	diplomatic crisis
terminal living	dying
hit/executive action	execution or assassination by government agents

What they say	What they mean
authentic reproduction	fake
full-figured	fat
dehired, selected out	fired
outplacement/decruitment/ constructive termination/ eliminating redundancies in the human-resources area	firing
open-space operative	gardener
pacification	genocide
active defence	invasion
correction facility	jail
account for	kill
unlawful or arbitrary deprivation of life	killing (US State Department)
enhanced dining facility	kitchen
categorical inaccuracy	lie
mail cover	mail opening
casualty	murder victim
selective ordnance	napalm
core rearrangement	nuclear accident
gadget	nuclear bomb
collateral damage	nuclear devastation

What they say	What they mean
episode	nuclear near-disaster
event	nuclear disaster
superprompt critical power excursion	nuclear meltdown
plausible denial	official lying
biosphere overload	overpopulation
recreational/arboreal amenity	park
permanent prehostility	peace (Pentagon)
underprivileged	poor
separate development	racialism
negative economic growth	recession
retrograde manoeuvre	retreat
civic amenity site	rubbish tip (GLC)
resource centre	school
human kinetics	school athletics
misunderstanding	screw-up
reconnaissance	search-and-destroy mission
retail facility/ customer-service outlet	shop
combat emplacement evacuator	shovel (US army)

What they say	What they mean
ground-displacement instrument	spade (civilian)
freedom fighter	terrorist
democratic	totalitarian
reforestation unit	tree
temporarily unsalaried	unemployed
preowned	used
personal hygiene centre	VD clinic
custom service manager	stewardess (airline)
freedom	subservience
revenue enhancement	taxes
advanced defence condition	war
ablutions facilities	washroom (British army)
climatic disturbances at the air-sea interface	waves (sea)

20 THE PRESS

'SSH . . . don't tell Diana but IT'S A GIRL', was the headline on my favourite press story of the year. Under the subheading 'Mirror Diary by Garth Gibbs', the report in the *Daily Mirror* of July 5, 1984 went on:

> . . . the sex was revealed during a routine medical scan – which monitors the growth and condition of the baby – on Princess Diana by Royal gynaecologist George Pinker . . .

Strange that, two months later, the *Mirror*'s baby princess had changed into . . . Prince Harry.

'Suzy', America's leading gossip columnist, reported in December 1984 that

> Elizabeth Taylor and Dennis Stein will wed sometime before March.

She added that Liz was

> Very, very serious . . .

about playboy Stein, who reminded her of her third husband, Mike Todd. The engagement was called off five weeks later.

> LINDA'S TELLY LOVE IS REAL
> *Dynasty* beauty Linda Evans is getting a new screen lover . . . her real life boyfriend Richard Chamberlain. The two sweethearts – rumoured to be planning an Easter wedding – will soon be swapping kisses in the TV soap opera.
>
> *'Sun', April 1984*

Linda Evans and Richard Chamberlain? Come off it!

> DI FLIES TO MARGARET
> *She will comfort ill Princess on holiday*

Princess Di and Prince Charles are planning to escort frail Princess Margaret on a get-well holiday in the sun. They are planning to fly to the Caribbean island of Mustique next month.

'News of the World', January 1985

The Royal couple went to Lichtenstein, then Jordan, instead.

LOW POUND WON'T SINK TAX CUTS
The Chancellor, Mr Nigel Lawson, still aims to deliver big tax cuts in the Budget, despite the continuing slide of the pound.

'Daily Mail', January 1985

Big tax cuts? You must be joking!

Some people have the idea that the *Spectator* is loyal to one particular party.

Charles Moore, editor, April 1985

Watford will this afternoon become the most laid back winners Wembley has ever seen . . .

Bob Driscoll, back-page lead in the 'Daily Star', May 1984, the day Everton beat Elton John's side 2–0.

Steve Jones, by contrast, has perhaps had too many races and too much travelling recently.

Cliff Temple, 'Sunday Times', preview to 1985 Mars London Marathon – the very day it was won, in course record time, by . . . Steve Jones

Mikhail Gorbachev is wildly tipped to succeed Soviet President Chernenko . . .

Press Association, December 1984

WE'VE GOT LUCAN

Most dishonest headline of the year, on the cover of 'YOU!', the 'Mail on Sunday' magazine, October 1984.

Of course they hadn't!

MRS THATCHER LEAVES FOR GANDHI FUNERAL: SECURITY GUARDS TOLD TO SHOOT ON SIGHT.

Headline in 'Glasgow Evening Times', January 1985

THATCHER READY TO LET £1 EQUAL $1

Headline in the 'Sunday Times', January 1985. As the paper hit the streets, the Treasury had already taken action to prop up sterling

Cheekiest headline of the year was the splash in the *Sunday Times*' sister paper, the *Sun*, in March 1985. It read:

CHARLES ACTS
IN
AIDS
SCARE

But the type was laid out in such a way that, when the *Sun* was on display with other papers on a newsagent's counter, the public would be most likely to see only:

CHARLES
IN
AIDS
SCARE

TEBBIT SET TO QUIT!
He decided before blast
Norman Tebbit, the 'iron man' Trade and Industry Secretary, is ready to quit the Cabinet.

It is a sensational decision that he had virtually taken even before the Brighton bomb atrocity in which he and his wife Margaret were seriously injured.

For Mr Tebbit's tough image had placed immense pressure on his wife and family . . . he told close friends last year he was thinking of going . . .

'Daily Star', October 1984

He was back at work in January 1985.

PA PARLY SNAP CORRECTION
COUNCIL Lords Nightlead
In page 4 please read in last paragraph: 'Londoners are the only people who are being denied the chance to run their own city.'
substituting 'run' for 'ruin'.

Press Association, June 1984

Hall of Infamy

SHERGAR IS ALIVE
Splash headline in 'Daily Express', March 1983

RUSSIA FIRM AND UNITED
Headline in 'The Times', London, December 1916

DEWEY DEFEATS TRUMAN
'Chicago Daily Tribune', election night 1948

JAP PLANE CARRIER AND FOUR U-BOATS SUNK
'Daily Express' headline on Pearl Harbor

300,000 SAY IT WITH MUSIC
'San Francisco Examiner' headline on the Rolling Stones' concert at Altamont, which erupted in frenzied violence with four dead and hundreds injured

TORIES NEED A MIRACLE NOW
Splash headline in the 'Observer', June 1970

NOW IT'S 'ODDS ON' CHARLES TO WED DAVINA
'Daily Express', February 1977

CARTER'S WINNING STREAK
The 'Spectator', November 1980, predicting a mauling for Ronald Reagan

ENGLISH DEFEAT

Splash headline in 'Diario Popular', Argentine newspaper, May 1982

I'M STAYING IN THE STREET SAYS LEN

'Daily Mirror' on court-troubled star Peter Adamson ('Len Fairclough'), 1983

TGWU GIVES VICTORY TO MEACHER

'The Times', September 1983, on why Michael Meacher would defeat Roy Hattersley for the Labour No. 2 job

TINY GRENADA DEFIES US

'Morning Star', October 1983

TEST TUBE BABY BOY!

The 'Sun' on the world's first test-tube baby – Louise Brown

BEATLES IN LIVE AID REUNION – Fab 3 Plus Julian

Screams the 'Sun' in a front page blockbuster story

GREAT HEADLINES

21 SPORT

Sport always provides some of the best Forked Tongues. From the promises of certain victory and the limp excuses after defeat to the faulty, fractured English of larger-than-life team-bosses, coaches and chairmen, it's an intense – and often false – world.

It was Olympic year, of course. And there were some classics.

There is certainly no reason to believe Mary Decker will do anything but win again against a much diluted field in the Olympic Games.
'Runners' World', August 1984, on the women's 3000m at Los Angeles

Again the absence of the Soviets makes this event a cinch for Mary Decker.
'The Runner', August 1984, on the same race

World Sporting Organisations must pool their efforts to protect the principle and ideals of the Olympic movement and to do everything possible for the games to remain a festival of peace and friendship.
Statement by the Soviet Olympic Committee, April 1984, shortly before they announced their boycott of Los Angeles

I don't think there is any question Zola Budd was in the wrong, I do hold her responsible for what happened.
Mary Decker, August 1984

The professionals disagreed. Allan Malamud of the *Los Angeles Herald-Examiner, wrote:*

Queen Mary Decker is wrong. The booing masses should look at the evidence.

Expect Martti Vainio to be in the thick of things.
'Runners' World' on the Finnish 10,000m entrant at Los Angeles

He was – in a way. He became the centre of a drug scandal. These profound predictions generally do invite disaster:

This club is on the march.
Malcolm Allison on Middlesborough, March 1984,

before he was sacked and the club made a bold bid for the third division . . . from the second

The next time I play Davis I'll stick it right up him. His luck is unbelievable and when we play again it will be a different story. I'll bury him.

Alex Higgins talking after a 5–1 defeat against Steve Davis in the Jameson Open Snooker Championship, October 1984. They met soon afterwards in the Coral UK Championships – Higgins lost

Of course, defeat brings its own heavy burden – of finding an excuse to explain what went wrong.

For two weeks I've been seeing the ball like a basketball. Today I couldn't find it.

Jimmy Connors, after losing 6–1, 6–1, 6–2 to John McEnroe at Wimbledon

Despite the scores I don't think there is that much disparity between the two sides.

David Gower, England cricket captain, after the First Test defeat (of five) against the West Indies, July 1984

Oh no? After their 3–19 defeat by Australia at Twickenham in November 1984, new England rugby captain Nigel Melville told why his men had lost:

We panicked.

Still on the oval code, the most misleading sporting headline of the year was surely this one from the *Western Mail* in March 1985. It read:

PENARTH IN SPIRITED FIGHT BACK

All was revealed, however, when readers looked below the large type to the score. It duly reported:

Llanelli 68pts, Penarth 3

There was some astonishing verbal cover-up from the BBC commentary team of David Coleman, Ron Pickering and Brendan Foster, covering the Mars 1985 London Marathon in April, when they did their level best to deny two significant features of the race – first that the leader for the first 13 miles, Chris Woodhouse of Derby, was a deliberate 'pacemaker' to try and set a record-breaking stride; and second, that the final leader and eventual winner, Steve Jones, stopped to relieve himself just outside the Tower of London.

On Woodhouse, who was seen running ahead of the field and exhorting the main contenders to quicken and catch him up, Brendan Foster said:

I think he just set off as he did to get a clear start.

Then he got rather abrasive:

This is a good lesson of what not to do in a marathon . . . I think he's having real problems containing his energy . . . all of his energy and enthusiasm has obviously taken him away from the leading group.

When Woodhouse mysteriously 'disappeared' from the race exactly at the half-way mark, and away from the cameras, David Coleman feigned total shock, horror and astonishment:

> Where is number 34? Can the helicopter camera pan forward and see if he is there . . . we still don't know whether he has been forced to drop out . . . he was certainly going well . . .

Rather more amusing were the lengths the BBC threesome went to to avoid revealing that the winner, Steve Jones, stopped to perform 'a bodily function' at the 22-mile mark at Traitors' Gate. 'Cramp' was the universal diagnosis. Said Pickering:

> Jones has gone and he's in trouble. Maybe that cramp is a serious affair.

Said Coleman:

> Brendan Foster said he might be trying to adjust his shorts which will of course be soaking wet with perspiration at this time.

Foster came closest to revealing the truth with the Freudian slip shortly afterwards:

> I think he's relieved now.

> Tom Watson today stands poised to rewrite the gold record books . . . Already recognised as the best player of his era, few among the crowds who thronged to the Old Course yesterday would bet against him taking a third successive Open Championship . . .
>
> *Peter Higgs, 'Mail on Sunday' at St Andrews, July 1984*

They should have. Ballesteros beat him.

> There was a lad standing in front of me when it happened and you know these old eyes of mine . . .
>
> *Joe Fagan, Liverpool manager, on the penalty refused to Everton in the Milk Cup Final*

However, 1984/85 proved yet again that it is the new 'armchair' sports which have really captured the public imagination, with their bloke-next-door heroes:

> One match, a load of Jocks put up this banner. 'Remember Bannockburn 1314,' it said. I'd no idea what it meant. It was only afterwards I found out it was some battle or other. I thought they were trying to slip some bird their 'phone number over the telly.
>
> *Eric Bristow, on an England* v. *Scotland darts match*

> I did him before and I'll do him again. I've had my problems of late, but Davis isn't unbeatable – that's rubbish! Just watch me go.
>
> *Alex Higgins, again, talking before losing to his arch-enemy in the £100,000 Coral UK Championships*

Steve Davis sounded forth in December 1984 on the physical demands of his sport:

> The toughest part of professional snooker is getting up and down from the chair. It really makes your leg-muscles ache. To stop the pain I do skipping and a press-up.

A press up, he was asked. One? He replied:

> I do two before a big match.

Hall of Infamy

We murdered them, 0–0.

Bill Shankly

Some people think football is a matter of life and death. It's not: it's a lot more serious than that.

Shankly again

We were doing great before they scored five freak goals.

Bert Head, manager of Crystal Palace

I was proud of them. They were hit by two sucker goals, and they showed tremendous character in the way they kept fighting back. I do not think they could have played much better..

Sir Alf Ramsey, 1973, after England were trounced 2–0 in Poland, on the way to being eliminated from the World Cup

Mind, I've been here during the bad times too. One year we came second.

Bob Paisley, manager of Liverpool, 1979

It's no good talking to me, lads – I'm not very experienced. I've only been fired once.

Ronnie Allen, then manager of Walsall

There's a hell of a lot of politics in football. I don't think Henry Kissinger would have lasted 48 hours at Old Trafford.

Tommy Docherty

THE SOCCER BOSS

22 BE YOUR OWN POLYGRAPH: 15 WAYS TO SPOT IF SOMEONE IS LYING

Polygraphs – lie detectors – are expensive and they can be lied to, too. Here, much cheaper (free with every copy of this book), is an infallible guide to the ways of telling when someone is lying to you.

The liar finds it relatively easy to control his or her tongue – but much more difficult to control the other parts of the body. These can soon give the Forked Tonguester away. Generally, when a person lies (and assuming, unlike politicians, salesmen and actors and actresses, they're not well practised at it) their heart beats faster and their blood pressure goes up, their throat constricts slightly, their eyes dance and their feet shuffle. Other bodily reactions have been monitored in recent academic research on psychology. Here are their findings in a nutshell.

Lack of eye contact Liars find it hard to look their victim straight in the eye. They may lower their head and then turn away sideways.

A higher-pitched voice From that lumpy, guilt-ridden throat.

Repetition Liars often repeat themselves because subconsciously they don't know if they've got the message across.

Hesitation The dead giveaway. If you ask a question and are met by a moment's silence . . . the liar's trying to come up with a good story.

Fewer hand-movements Liars cut down on the number of normal hand-gestures. It's in the subconscious: they're worrying they'll use the wrong gesture and give the game away.

Brief look of despair Watch for the split-second giveaway. Professor Paul Ekman of the University of California at San Francisco found with practice his researchers could spot 'microexpressions' of deceit lasting as little as 1/24 of a second. They include a 'squelched' face and a sudden, brief look of despair.

The one-shoulder shrug Liars give a characteristic shrug of the hand, with a brief but detectable lift of one shoulder, in the middle of their spiel. It's their body trying to disclaim itself from the verbal bluff.

Hand-to-face touches There are other involuntary signs of deceit. In the *mouth cover*, his hand is trying to stop his sleight of tongue. The *nose touch* is a mystery, but liars always do it.

Head nodding He's betraying his own doubts and his insincerity.

The prolonged smile A liar will often put on a plastic smile. Look hard. If it doesn't go to the eyes, and if it lasts more than four or five seconds, he's trying to deceive you.

The crooked face In trying to feign shock, grief or delight, a liar tries to bring all his facial muscles into concert. If he's not a trained actor, he will always fail. Watch for the unevenly raised eyebrows, asymmetric facial lines, the crooked smile.

The split-second gap The liar can never properly time his words and gestures correctly. Watch: if he bangs the table or points a finger accusingly, is there a time lag before he adjusts his face to feign the requisite anger?

Coughing Watch, too, for the liar's nervous cough. Chm! Just like that.

Distance Liars often show their guilt by taking an extra pace away from you, showing that they're embarrassed to be close while being so false.

The soft shoe shuffle Above all, WATCH HIS FEET. These are the furthest bodily parts from the brain and the most difficult to control. Liars often shuffle and move from foot to foot quite uncontrollably – why else should we call dishonest people 'shifty'?

Four Golden Rules for Would-be Deceivers

1 LOOK your victim straight in the eye.

2 TALK in a deep, controlled voice at normal speed. Don't hesitate or repeat yourself.

3 REMEMBER your hands. Use these carefully to emphasise your fibs or alibis. *Never* raise them higher than your chest. *Never* touch your nose, mouth or hair.

4 KEEP your feet still.

Good luck! But, if you really want to be a successful liar, do it through a five-foot wall, sitting or lying down – or, best of all, over the telephone.

23 NO. 1 LIES

'I have often wished I had time to cultivate modesty,' said Edith Sitwell, 'but I am too busy thinking about myself.' Winston Churchill used to observe: 'It is no part of my case that I am always right.' However, perhaps the most pertinent self-comment came from Katherine Anne Porter, American essayist and *femme fatale*: 'My life has been incredible. I don't believe a word of it.'

It has been quite a year for No. 1 lies – those about the ego. The mighty self. Number One.

No. 1 lies fall into two categories: (1) the pomposity and conceit of braggarts and big mouths, and (2) the humility and self-effacement of genuinely humbler men and women. Let's take the first category – the boastful – first:

> I started really long hair for men, so I'm finishing it. *Mine* is this year's new look.
>
> *Boy George on his shorn locks, January 1985*

> Now my hair can be as *gorgeous* as the rest of me.
>
> *Olympic gold medallist Steve Lundquist in his new career advertising Sassoon anti-dandruff shampoo*

Thank goodness that most seem to fib in the other direction – whether or not you can believe that that's what they really think.

> Anyone can do what I have done.
>
> *George Michael of Wham!, April 1985, after barnstorming tour of China*

> I've never accepted the idea of being a sex symbol. It makes me laugh just to think about it. I'm just one of the blokes who likes to watch West Ham and have a few

I'm just another working mum.

Joan Collins, April 1984

I look like Porky Pig.

Simon Le Bon, on some publicity stills, April 1984

drinks with my friends.

David Essex, November 1984

I can tell you that there are many occasions when I'd happily swap them for something smaller.

Samantha Fox, 'Page Three Girl of the Year', July 1984

Not everyone has such a low opinion of themselves, of course. Flamboyant London barrister Rudy Narayan, *enfant terrible* of the legal establishment, announced in April 1984 that he was leaving his barrister's chambers to become a solicitor. He said:

> What disgusts me is that a man as brilliant and good-looking as myself should earn far less than solicitors of much less competence.

In November he had to swallow humble pie – well, a little, at least. He failed his exams.

Meanwhile, Cataya Sassoon, who caused a sensation in California in 1984 by marrying at 15, said on making her first film, *Tuff Turf*:

> I am not a Brooke Shields or a Christie Brinkley. I think I'm more a Meryl Streep.

Not bad for a 16-year-old with no formal training whose acting career had progressed to a dozen lines or so in a B movie. The established stars, by contrast, tend to play down their charms.

I was named one magazine's favourite sex symbol. It seemed so funny to me because I have these broad shoulders and was always such a skinny person.

Linda Evans, 'Krystle Carrington' in 'Dynasty', December 1984

My wife made me a jock strap. A *little* grey thing.
Charlton Heston

Any well-built 5′ 7½″ tall girl could do it. Seriously she could. Wait till those make-up people get through with you for two hours and no girl would recognise herself.
Deborah Shelton, 'Mandy Winger' in Dallas, on how anyone could become a soap sex siren, February 1985

I do have a very crooked face. One side is up, the other down. The left side of my jaw is longer than my right. I'm gap-toothed. My features are really strange. They are just a mess.
Lauren Hutton

They really do hate what they see in the mirror.

I hardly look in the mirror these days and when I do I cannot see much. I need to wear my glasses now.
Brigitte Bardot, now 50

It was so weird taking the braces off my teeth because I looked in the mirror and wanted them back on! They're like a decoration. You get used to them and when you've lost them you think, 'Oh, I'm so plain.'
Heather Locklear, Sammy Jo in 'Dynasty' and Stacy Sheridan in 'T. J. Hooker'

Ah, but all these people have *achieved* something, haven't they?

I know what's important to me
and it's nothing I've achieved.
Paul McCartney, October 1984

How can I feel like a film star when I do my own ironing?
Meryl Streep

Hall of Infamy

I am not a superstar. I am a mega-superstar.
Jack Nicholson

I am good-looking, intelligent, articulate, arrogant, and an artist.
Marvyn Gaye, soul singer

Broadway has been very good to me – but then I've been very good to Broadway.
Ethel Merman, singer

It's bloody tough being a legend.
Ron Atkinson, Manchester United manager

Of course I wouldn't just like to be involved with the bits and bobs of politics. I would like to be Prime Minister.
Kevin Keegan

I am in a great state of euphoria. I have just given the finest party political broadcast in history.
Harold Wilson, 1976, quoted by Richard Crossman

I am quite willing now to relinquish the supreme-being title.
David Bowie, August 1983

I am just an ordinary fellow, with ordinary obligations, and a family.
Neil Kinnock

I'm a good wine, but a bad year.

Paul Newman, told by his wife Joanne that 'men are like a good wine – they improve with age'

We're just a bunch of crummy musicians.

George Harrison on the Beatles

Usually I turn the radio off when I hear my voice. It nauseates me so much.

Lyndsey de Paul

I keep hoping people will realise how dull I am. Then perhaps they'll stop bothering me.

Robert Redford

My feet are tiny. They couldn't grow in all that shade.

Dolly Parton

I get tired of films. When you remember that one of the greatest film stars was Lassie and she was a dog, there is no great stroke in it. I'm just like a plumber doing a service.

Robert Mitchum, September 1983

I know it sounds terrible but my Oscar for *Annie Hall* didn't mean anything to me. I just don't think they know what they are doing.

Woody Allen

24 DOUBLETHINK

'If I ever utter an oath again, may my soul be blasted to eternal damnation,' declared George Benard Shaw. 'I have always thought that every woman should marry, and no man,' said Benjamin Disraeli. 'I am fond of children (except boys),' wrote Lewis Carroll.

This is a chapter about double standards. What George Orwell, the personality of 1984 himself, styled *doublethink* – the capacity to hold two diametrically opposed views and at the same time to believe passionately in both of them.

And, yes, there was a fair amount of doublethink during the year. For example, there was Mr Robert McCartney, QC. Seeing that a journalist had failed to stand for *God Save the Queen* at an Official Unionist Party meeting, Mr McCartney chastised him as follows:

> **** off out of here if you can't observe the niceties.

Also in Ireland, Wexford Fianna Fail TD Dr Hugh Byrne, at a protest meeting in May 1984, launched into a bitter tirade against An Bord Telecom, accusing it of 'disgraceful behaviour' and 'extortion of the worst order'. He declared:

> There has not been one iota of change since An Bord Telecom took over – and if there has been, it has been for the worse.

> I'm very anti-violence.
>
> *Clint Eastwood, movie shoot-out king, January 1985*

Perhaps the blackest show of doublethink during the year came in April 1985, when Mrs Edna Healey, the wife of Labour's former deputy leader, went into hospital for a private hip replacement operation. She claimed:

> I was forced into going private.

While insisting:

> I disapprove in principle of private medicine.

'In principle' meaning, of course, that everyone else should be made to go on the NHS.

> I can be faithful despite what some people say. I'm sure I've been faithful for more than a year . . . but I think when you go on the road you kind of let things like being faithful go to pieces.
>
> *Mick Jagger, February 1985*

> I have been up and down and round about and I never look backward.
>
> *Katharine Hepburn, interview in the 'Mail on Sunday', November 1984*

> Unless you are an absolute moron, you have regrets. Sometimes when I go to the sea and watch the birds fly off in twos and I drive off alone, I wonder, did I make a mistake?
>
> *Katharine Hepburn, later in same interview*

In December 1984 fellow-members of the ITV show *Surprise, Surprise* planned to catch Cilla Black out in front of the camera. She discovered the plot, was furious and stopped it. Said lovable Cilla, not one to shrink from surprising others 'live':

> I was caught out once before and I didn't like it one bit. I don't think the viewers want to see surprises pulled on me.

After Prince Charles had given a no-holds-barred interview

to Barbara Walters in November 1984, other journalists were keen to get hold of Miss Walters to find out more about the encounter. A spokesman replied:

Miss Walters doesn't give interviews.

In July 1984, on assuming command at Mirror Newspapers, 'Captain Bob', while not interfering editorially, announced a 'We Back Britain' policy and promised that the paper would promote what was best about the country, instead of griping, knocking, and so on. Indeed, the *Daily Mirror* began to carry the masthead slogan 'Forward with Britain'. Somebody didn't tell the sports department. One of their first headlines under Mr Maxwell was on the Headingley Test and read:

ENGLAND
Rubbish
Incompetent
Pathetic

It is one thing to kill your wife. It is quite another to cut off her finger which was the only way to remove the ring.

Airline pilot Peter Hogg, who was trapped as his wife's killer by identification of her ring. He received three years for manslaughter in March 1985

Y'know you can't expect people to ballot other people out of a job.

Tony Benn, MP, twisting logic on BBC TV, January 1985. He was against a ballot for the miners, although he had been standing in parliamentary elections for years

Michael Nader, who plays Dex Dexter in the TV soap

Dynasty, was somewhat bitchy about his fellow-star Joan Collins in January 1985, accusing her of double standards on the set. Said Nader:

> In one scene where I had to slap her, she kept telling me beforehand: 'Michael, darling, be careful, you know how easily I bruise.' When her turn came to hit me, she rocked my head backwards and nearly knocked it off my neck.

On his otherwise sweetness-and-light visit to Britain in December 1984, Kremlin heir-apparent Mikhail Gorbachev was knocked off balance by a question from Conservative MP Norman St John Stevas about the treatment of the Church in the Soviet Union. Said an angry Gorbachev:

> I could give you a few facts about human rights in the United Kingdom. For example, you persecute entire communities, entire nationalities.

Not as in Russia, of course.

Also in December 1984, escaped train-robber Ronald Biggs, now in Brazil, went into the nightclub business and said he would be very particular about his clientele. At the club's opening he announced:

> There will be no women of ill-repute or violent crooks allowed in this place.

In the same month Broadmoor killer and one-time ruthless gang boss Ronnie Kray ordered a £300 suit for his prison wedding to 28-year-old sweetheart, Elaine Mildener. It was stolen. Said Ronnie:

> I just don't know what the world is coming to.

Hall of Infamy

I don't want a cabinet of yes-men. They are no good to a Prime Minister.

Margaret Thatcher

You know, we really have to get those Turkeys out of there.

Geraldine Ferraro, talking on Cyprus in her first Congressional foreign affairs speech, 1979

I'm learning about money. I'm learning how to wield a vacuum and how to put the garbage out and how to cook, and how to go to the supermarket. I've never been doing better in my entire life.

Joan Kennedy, after her split from husband Senator Edward Kennedy, March 1982

She's just like the lady next door.

Easterhouse (Glasgow) housewife on Princess Diana

I'm basically a home body at heart.

Margaret Trudeau

It was so cold that I almost got married.

Shelley Winters on a winter-sports holiday

10 came on television the other night and I just had to switch it off.

Bo Derek

Ideally I would like to have Candice Bergen's face on my body.

Racquel Welch

No, I'm not disappointed – I'm actually rather pleased in a way. This truly is a remarkable result.

Shirley Williams, losing at Crosby, June 1983

I have always been so frightfully proper.

Mandy Rice-Davies, who scandalised Britain in the Profumo affair

I'm a real librarian at heart – very shy.

Bette Midler

If I were a teenager today, I'd probably be a pink-haired punk.

Mary Whitehouse

I still don't have any confidence.

Bette Midler again

Oh God – how I wish I were Liza Minnelli.

Racquel Welch

CLASSIC FEMALE LINES

Hall of Infamy

I never really cared about acting.
Robert Redford

I have no interest in making films.
Marlon Brando

I'm a realist.
Pulp Western king J. T. Edson

I still ride my bike to the paper shop in the mornings.
Boy George, November 1983

A trade-union leader has one obligation above all else, to put the members first.
Arthur Scargill, November 1981

I intend to open up this country to democracy and anyone who is against that, I will jail, I will crush.
President João Baptista Figueiredo of Brazil, on taking office, 1979

Sure we've got plenty of leads – but they don't lead anywhere.
Irish detective on the hunt for Shergar, May 1983

I don't think people mind a little downright rudeness or prejudice.
Prince Philip

My burning desire is to be a monk.
Richard Harris

I want to earn an honest living.
Ronald Biggs

Kissing Marilyn Monroe was like kissing Adolf Hitler!
Tony Curtis

Overexposing Ronald Reagan as President is like overexposing Bo Derek.
Senator Paul Laxalt

Diana had to marry somebody.
Earl Spencer

I am no playboy. What is a playboy anyway?
Prince Andrew

Playboy has crusaded for a long time on behalf of women.
Hugh Hefner, 1971

They say *Penthouse* exploits women. The truth is, women exploit *Penthouse*.
Bob Guccione, 1979

Maybe I'm a frustrated army officer.
Mick Jagger

CLASSIC MALE LINES

25 LIKE *DALLAS*, WITH BALLS

'Driving on the Houston freeway is more dangerous. I'd take my chances on the launchpad any day,' said Kathryn Sullivan, 33, the first American woman to walk in space, in December 1984. 'The last thing I want is my children to be dishonest. It's nicer being an honest person,' said fugitive train-robber. Ronnie Biggs. 'I know I'm going to be President,' said Senator Gary Hart. Well, not this time.

Here they are – the craziest one-liners of the year.

> He should allow himself to be as funny in public as he is in private.
>
> *Mrs Joan Mondale*

What do you mean? In public he's hilarious!

> I don't tolerate fools gladly. In fact, I don't tolerate fools, period.
>
> *Mark Thatcher*

No comment, period.

> I don't think being married to me has helped her at all. On the contrary, it has probably knocked her back a couple of years.
>
> *Andrew Lloyd-Webber on Sarah Brightman*

When punks Sharon Brown and Kevin Thickett married at Poplar Register Office, London, the bride wore all black and had her head half-shaved. The groom was also in black, but his hair was dyed bright red. He explained afterwards:

I didn't want to look a wally.

> Snooker is just like *Dallas*, with balls.
>
> *Steve Davis*

I've given up chasing women. I'd rather stay in bed with a good book.

Rod Stewart

This is going to be a very special year for me.

Ronnie Kray, celebrating the onset of 1985 in Broadmoor

On a boys' night out after a game the most I'll have is seven or eight pints of lager. That to me isn't being drunk.

Charlie Nicholas, Arsenal soccer star

Boxing? I hate it. Who could possibly enjoy being knocked about?

Joe Bugner

Sometimes I feel like a heavyweight boxer coming out of retirement and not really wanting to go through it all again at 35. Snooker is a young man's game now.

Alex Higgins

I could not be a teacher myself. I don't have the skill or the personality.

Sir Keith Joseph

I am prepared to consider what my membership wants.

Arthur Scargill

If people don't like Marxism, they should blame the British Museum.

Soviet heir-apparent Mikhail Gorbachev visiting the reading room where the father of Communism did his research

You are safer in a chemical plant than in your own home.

Warren Anderson, chairman of Union Carbide, after the Bhopal blast

William Shakespeare wrote for the masses. If he were alive today, he'd probably be the chief scriptwriter on *Dallas*.

Rupert Murdoch

My one regret in life is that I am not someone else.
Woody Allen

Would you ever buy a used car from me?
John De Lorean

I deserve a hell of a lot more respect than I get.
John McEnroe

Fashion is dead. There is no such thing as fashion.
Jasper Conran, designer

I'm amazed at Australia's size. I thought Melbourne was just down the road from Sydney.
George Michael of Wham! His fellow-singer, Andy Ridgeley, said: 'Geography was never one of George's strong points.'

To me he's a caring, considerate, gentle man and I'm prepared to wait for him as long as it takes for him to be released.
Elaine Mildener, 28-year-old wife of Broadmoor inmate Ronnie Kray. Former fiancée Stella Burnett, 54, said: 'He'll be the perfect husband – as long as he stays in Broadmoor.'

I sometimes wonder if we're not all better off inside than in the outside world. It's become an absolute jungle.
Ronnie Kray